Table of Contents

I0427785

To the Congress of the United States

I am pleased to transmit the 2012 *National Drug Control Strategy*, which follows through on the commitment made by my Administration to chart a new course in our efforts to reduce illicit drug use and its consequences in the United States. The balanced approach outlined in the Administration's inaugural *National Drug Control Strategy* has yielded significant results, which are detailed in the following pages.

Our Nation still faces serious drug-related challenges, however. Too many Americans need treatment for substance use disorders but do not receive it. Prescription drug abuse continues to claim American lives, and those who take drugs and drive threaten safety on our Nation's roadways. Young people's perceptions of the risks of drug use have declined over the past decade, and research suggests that this often predicts future increases in drug use. There is still much left to do to reform our justice system and break the cycle of drug use and crime. Our commitment to work with partner nations must remain steadfast to reduce drug production, trafficking, and related transnational threats.

Based upon the progress we have achieved over the past three years, I am confident we can address these challenges through concerted action along the entire spectrum of prevention, early intervention, treatment, recovery support, criminal justice reform, law enforcement, and international cooperation. However, we must match our commitment with the appropriate resources.

Illicit drug use in America contributed to an estimated $193 billion in crime, health, and lost productivity costs in 2007, the year for which the most recent estimate is available. In today's challenging economic environment, we cannot afford such a drain on our economy and public resources. While difficult budget decisions must be made at all levels of government, we must ensure continued support for policies and programs that reduce drug use and its enormous costs to American society. In doing so, we will not only strengthen our economy but also sustain the national character and spirit that has made the United States a world leader.

I look forward to continuing to work with the Congress and Federal, state, local, tribal, and territorial leaders, international partners, and the American people in this important endeavor.

Barack Obama
The White House

Preface from Director Kerlikowske

The Administration's inaugural *National Drug Control Strategy*, published in 2010, represented a new direction in our efforts to reduce illicit drug use and its consequences in the United States. The spirit and substance of that *Strategy* reflected the unique nature in which it was developed—at the President's direction, the Office of National Drug Control Policy (ONDCP) engaged in an unprecedented consultation process, collecting input from Congress, Federal, state, local, tribal, territorial, and international partners, nongovernmental organizations, and the American public. Upon release of the *Strategy*, I committed this office to oversee its implementation with the same rigor and transparency that marked its development. This document, the 2012 *National Drug Control Strategy*, incorporates input from a diverse range of stakeholders while also reflecting implementation progress as reported by dozens of Federal agencies regarding the action items for which they are responsible.

This *Strategy* reflects new developments in our efforts to reduce drug use and its consequences, but our goal remains the same: a 15 percent reduction in the rate of drug use and similar reductions in drug use consequences over the course of five years (2010-2015). To achieve this goal, we will continue to pursue a balanced approach that brings all sectors of society together in a national effort to improve public health and safety. Through community-based programs and early intervention in health care settings, we will work to prevent illicit drug use and addiction before their onset and bring more Americans in need of treatment into contact with the appropriate level of care. We will continue to build on the Administration's progress in reforming the justice system, ensuring that laws are applied fairly and effectively—protecting public safety while also ensuring that drug-involved offenders have the opportunity to end their drug use and rebuild their lives. We will continue to counter drug production and trafficking within the United States and will implement new strategies to secure our borders against illicit drug flows. And we will work with international partners to reduce drug production and trafficking and strengthen rule of law, democratic institutions, citizen security, and respect for human rights around the world.

Achieving the progress detailed in the following pages would not have been possible without the support of Congress, and such support will remain essential as we seek to reduce drug use and its consequences in America throughout 2012. I thank the Congress—and individuals all across the country—for their continued partnership in building a healthier and safer America.

R. Gil Kerlikowske
Director of National Drug Control Policy

Introduction

In his message to Congress in the Administration's first *National Drug Control Strategy,* the President affirmed that "…a well-crafted strategy is only as successful as its implementation. To succeed, we will need to rely on the hard work, dedication, and perseverance of every concerned American." For 3 years this principle has guided the Administration's efforts to include all sectors of American society in a comprehensive national effort to reduce illicit drug use and its consequences. The Administration's first *Strategy* included 106 action items to be undertaken by Federal agencies in partnership with state, local, tribal, and international counterparts to prevent illicit drug use in our communities; intervene early in the health care system; strengthen drug treatment services and support the millions of Americans in recovery; break the cycle of drug use, crime, and incarceration; disrupt domestic drug production and trafficking; strengthen international partnerships; and improve drug-related information systems. The 2011 *National Drug Control Strategy* built upon this policy framework, addressed several important legislative developments, and added a focus on the needs of special populations such as college and university students, women and families, and military members, veterans, and their families.

Progress has been achieved in a number of important areas during the past year. In 2011, the Administration announced the release of the *National Prevention Strategy*, which includes substance use prevention as part of a comprehensive plan to help increase the number of Americans who are healthy at every stage of life. Screening, Brief Intervention, and Referral to Treatment services continued to reach more Americans in the health care system, and more patients in health centers across the Nation were provided access to substance use disorder treatment services. Drug courts and other innovative criminal justice programs offered more drug-involved offenders the opportunity to undergo treatment as an alternative to incarceration. The Administration developed strategies to reduce the flow of drugs across both the northern and southern borders, while also addressing the threat of drug production and trafficking within the United States. Internationally, the United States strengthened bonds with partner nations, working to reduce the flow of illicit drugs to the United States while also developing a new *Strategy to Combat Transnational Organized Crime* that addresses the role of the drug trade in broader threats to national security. Concurrently, the Administration has worked to enhance data collection, fill information gaps, and improve the relevance of data systems in the national effort to reduce drug use and its consequences.

The Administration also maintained its focus on the key issues of drugged driving and prescription drug abuse. The President drew much-needed attention to the issue of drugged driving by declaring December *National Impaired Driving Prevention Month* in both 2010 and 2011. Throughout the year, the Administration advanced initiatives to improve public awareness, enhance law enforcement training, improve screening methodologies, and collect more comprehensive data to support policy-making.

In response to a prescription drug abuse problem designated as an epidemic by the Centers for Disease Control and Prevention (CDC), in 2011, the Administration moved forward with the implementation of the *Prescription Drug Abuse Prevention Plan*. The Plan includes four pillars to reduce prescription drug abuse: education, monitoring, proper medication disposal, and enforcement. The passage by Congress of the Secure and Responsible Drug Disposal Act of 2010 will greatly assist in the implementation of the

Prescription Drug Abuse Prevention Plan, allowing the Drug Enforcement Administration (DEA) to implement regulations on the disposal of controlled substances by ultimate users, long term care facilities, and other authorized persons. While the rulemaking process proceeds, DEA is working with its Federal, state, local, and tribal partners to support communities in their efforts to safely dispose unused prescription drugs through its National Prescription Drug Take Back Initiative.

Important steps have been taken to address the unique needs of special populations affected by the drug problem. With regard to college and university students, the Administration has partnered with college and university leaders to advance prevention, early intervention, treatment, and recovery initiatives on campuses across the country. The Administration initiated the VetCorps program to recruit veterans to serve in community coalitions across the country, providing economic opportunities, housing, health care, and drug prevention and treatment services for veterans and their families. And the Administration continued to provide funding support for family-based treatment and forged new partnerships to improve policies and programs responsive to the unique needs of women and families affected by drug use.

The following chapters provide progress updates on implementation of the 2010 and 2011 *National Drug Control Strategy*. In each chapter, action items appear in italics, with the original action item numbers from the 2010 Strategy following in parentheses. As detailed in the pages that follow, significant progress has been achieved in many important areas of the *National Drug Control Strategy*, but America still faces a serious drug problem that requires sustained focus and concerted action from all sectors of American society. For example, findings from the 2011 Monitoring the Future study indicate that while illicit drug use among teens did not change significantly between 2010 and 2011, there have been significant increases in past-month use since 2006, mostly driven by increased rates of marijuana use. Between 2006 and 2011, past-month use of any illicit drug among 10th graders increased from 16.8 percent to 19.2 percent. During the same time period, past-month use of marijuana among 10th graders increased from 14.2 percent to 17.6 percent.[1]

In pursuing the *National Drug Control Strategy* in 2012, we will remain flexible and adaptable, responding to new threats as they emerge. For example, the Monitoring the Future study also revealed the shocking finding that in 2011 one in nine high school seniors had used "synthetic marijuana" (synthetic cannabinoids commonly marketed as "herbal incense" in products such as "Spice" or "K2") during the past year, meaning that synthetic cannabinoids are now the second most frequently used illicit drug, after marijuana, among high school seniors.[2] These substances can cause serious adverse health effects; calls to Poison Control Centers relating to synthetic cannabinoids reached 6,890 in 2011—more than double the number received in all of 2010.[3] The Administration has responded rapidly to the emerging threat of synthetic drugs, convening Federal agencies and nongovernmental organizations to develop a coordinated response. DEA has taken emergency action to temporarily control five synthetic cannabinoids and three synthetic cathinones that are common ingredients in these dangerous substances. In December 2011, the House of Representatives passed legislation that would ban several synthetic drugs, including some that are marketed as "bath salts." After passage in the House, the bill was referred to the Senate. The Administration will continue to work with Congress to address the synthetic drug threat throughout 2012.

Moving forward, it is vitally important that we support efforts to address a drug problem that threatens public health and safety and impedes education, innovation, and economic competitiveness in the United States. By applying our resources efficiently in pursuit of the goals that follow, our Nation can reduce illicit drug use and its consequences. The chapters that follow depict the progress made to date and reaffirm the Administration's commitment to building a healthy, safe, and prosperous future for America.

National Drug Control Strategy Goals to Be Attained by 2015

Goal 1: Curtail illicit drug consumption in America

    1a. Decrease the 30-day prevalence of drug use among 12- to 17-year-olds by 15 percent

    1b. Decrease the lifetime prevalence of 8th graders who have used drugs, alcohol, or tobacco by 15 percent

    1c. Decrease the 30-day prevalence of drug use among young adults aged 18–25 by 10 percent

    1d. Reduce the number of chronic drug users by 15 percent

Goal 2: Improve the public health and public safety of the American people by reducing the consequences of drug abuse

    2a. Reduce drug-induced deaths by 15 percent

    2b. Reduce drug-related morbidity by 15 percent

    2c. Reduce the prevalence of drugged driving by 10 percent

Data Sources: SAMHSA's National Survey on Drug Use and Health (1a, 1c); Monitoring the Future (1b); What Americans Spend on Illegal Drugs (1d); Centers for Disease Control and Prevention (CDC) National Vital Statistics System (2a); SAMHSA's Drug Abuse Warning Network drug-related emergency room visits, and CDC data on HIV infections attributable to drug use (2b); National Survey on Drug Use and Health and National Highway Traffic Safety Administration (NHTSA) roadside survey (2c)

Chapter 1. Strengthen Efforts to Prevent Drug Use in Our Communities

Introduction

Drug use, including the abuse of prescription medications and underage drinking, significantly affects the health and well-being of the Nation's youth and young adults. Substance use affects academic performance and military preparedness and is linked to crime, motor vehicle crashes and fatalities, lost productivity, and increased health care costs. [4,5,6,7,8] Stopping use before it begins can increase an individual's chances of living a longer, healthier, and more productive life. Put simply, drug prevention saves lives and cuts long-term costs. Recent research has shown that each dollar invested in an evidence-based prevention program can reduce costs related to substance use disorders by an average of $18. [9]

As discussed previously, while overall youth drug use did not statistically change between 2010 and 2011, past-month use of any illicit drug among 10th graders increased from 16.8 percent in 2006 to 19.2 percent in 2011. [10] Marijuana typically drives the trends in estimates of any illicit drug use, and, accordingly, past-month use of marijuana among 10th graders increased from 14.2 percent in 2006 to 17.6 percent in 2011. [11] In addition, there continues to be a decline in the perceived risk of marijuana use among teens. [12] This is troubling, as research shows drug use trends among youth typically increase one to two years after a weakening of the perceived danger of using drugs. [13] One possible influence on this observed trend in drug use and perception of risk is the decreased exposure of youth to prevention messages and the presence of messages and policies that downplay the consequences of drug use. [14] While the Administration supports ongoing research into determining what components of the marijuana plant can be used as medicine, to date, neither the FDA nor the Institute of Medicine has found the marijuana plant itself to meet the modern standard for safe or effective medicine for any condition. The Administration also recognizes that legalizing marijuana would not provide the answer to any of the health, social, youth education, criminal justice, and community quality of life challenges associated with drug use.

America's young people deserve every opportunity to live up to their full potential. Research shows that exposure to effective community-based drug prevention programming in school settings, for example, improves their chances to do so. [15,16] Evidence-based substance use prevention is therefore among the highest drug policy priorities of the Obama Administration. In keeping with the President's goal of winning the future and investing in what makes America stronger, we must focus our limited Federal resources to support state and local efforts to stop drug use and underage drinking before they start. The Substance Abuse Prevention and Treatment Block Grant (SAPTBG) and discretionary programs, like Health and Human Services (HHS) Strategic Prevention Framework-State Incentive Grants and the collaborative HHS—Department of Education Safe Schools/Healthy Students Program demonstrate the Administration's commitment to prevention. The most recent SAPTBG data, for example, show state-level changes in the perception of the risk of harm from substance use among youth ages 12-17 in almost half of the states, while 19 states showed improvement among those ages 18 or older. In addition,

27 states achieved a decrease in past 30-day alcohol use among underage youth.[17] The Safe Schools/ Healthy Students Program draws on the best practices of education, juvenile justice, law enforcement, and mental-health systems to provide integrated resources for prevention and early intervention services for children and youth. The most recent data indicate that 51.9, 58.3, and 55.2 percent of the 2007, 2008, and 2009 grant cohorts, respectively, reported a decrease in the percentage of students reporting current (past 30 days) marijuana use.[18]

In addition to the youth programs mentioned previously, as our young people enter the workplace and others remain engaged in workforce, it is important to ensure a drug-free workplace. The consequences of illicit drug use in America's workforce include job-related accidents and injuries, absenteeism, health care costs, and lost productivity.[19] Workplace programs that provide clear policies regarding drug use; offer prevention and education opportunities for employers and supervisors; conduct drug testing to detect and deter use; and support referral and treatment for those who have substance use disorders can play a large role in reducing the demand for drugs throughout our Nation and in helping drug users get into treatment. These programs provide employees with the opportunity to self-identify and get help. Often, such programs give employees an opportunity to return to the same job, or a similar job in the same industry, thereby creating an incentive to succeed in their recovery and resume a fulfilling career. Consequently, drug-free workplace programs are beneficial for our labor force, employers, families, and communities in general.

Accomplishments

A National Prevention System Must be Grounded at the Community Level

Collaborate with States to Support Communities (1.1.B.) In March 2011, the Substance Abuse and Mental Health Services Administration (SAMHSA) issued 46 grants for its Strategic Prevention Enhancement program to allow states and tribes to assess their current prevention infrastructure to identify gaps in capacity and, based on findings, develop a long-term, data driven plan to restructure, enhance, and/or further strengthen their prevention systems to better meet the needs of their communities.

Spread Prevention to the Workplace (1.1.C.) The Department of Labor's Job Corps conducted 12 interactive multi-session drug prevention workshops and launched an online program for Job Corps participants to encourage healthy drug-free lifestyles. As part of the National Prescription Drug Take Back Initiative sponsored by the DEA, 506 pounds of unwanted and/or expired medications were collected on October 28, 2011 from Federal employees based in 14 Federal worksites throughout the Washington, DC area.

Prevention Efforts Must Encompass the Range of Settings in Which Young People Grow Up

Strengthen the Drug Free Communities Support Program (1.2.A.) In August 2011, the Administration announced $12.3 million in new DFC Support Program grants to 87 communities and 20 new DFC Mentoring grants. In addition, nearly $76 million in continuation grants were awarded to 607 currently funded DFC coalitions and 12 DFC Mentoring coalitions. In this grant cycle, 74 percent of the new competing awards serve urban areas. This reflects a significant rebalancing among the types of communities

VetCorps: Veterans Helping Veterans

Since 2001, more than two million troops have deployed to Afghanistan or Iraq—with many service members deploying multiple times.[21] These men and women join the more than 22 million military veterans in the United States today.[22] Multiple deployments can sometimes strain service members as well as their families.[23] The Veterans and Military Families Corps (VetCorps) project is being administered by Community Anti-Drug Coalitions of America (CADCA) and conducted in partnership with the National Guard Bureau's Prevention, Treatment and Outreach Program with

Robert Velasco II, Acting CEO of the Corporation for National and Community Service, swears in new VetCorps members at the CADCA National Leadership Forum, February 9, 2012.

funding assistance from the Corporation for National & Community Service. The aim of the project is to recruit 100 AmeriCorps and AmeriCorps VISTA members, particularly veterans (including inactive National Guard and Reserve members), and place them in CADCA community coalitions in 29 states in the first year. The program seeks to provide access to health care—with an emphasis on substance abuse prevention and treatment—and housing and employment to veterans and military families. According to CADCA's Chairman and CEO, retired Gen. Arthur T. Dean, "We developed VetCorps to improve the overall quality of life for veterans and military families, particularly National Guard and Reserve members who do not benefit from services readily available on military bases. We will be using the valuable skills and knowledge of veterans to help other veterans in the community."

funded by the DFC Support Program: Of the 718 grantees that currently make up the DFC program, 43 percent are urban and 47 percent are rural communities. In addition, Native American populations are served by 8 percent of the total DFC awards. A national evaluation of the DFC Support Program found that youth substance use has declined significantly in DFC communities.[20]

Revamp and Reenergize the National Youth Anti-Drug Media Campaign (1.2.B.) Since 2005, there has been a significant public investment in developing the widely-recognized "Above the Influence" (ATI) brand, a campaign that has been found by independent scientific analyses to be effective, relevant to youth, and instrumental to drug prevention efforts in communities across the country.[24,25,26] Since 2010, the National Youth Anti-Drug Media Campaign has worked directly with youth-serving organizations (e.g., DFC Support Program grantees, Boys & Girls Clubs of America, YMCAs, Students Against Destructive Decisions chapters) to increase teen and community-level participation with the ATI brand. Further, the Campaign has built a strong online and social media presence, with a Facebook fan base of over 500,000 teens (adding at a rate of approximately 4,000 ATI friends per week). Unfortunately, despite evidence of its effectiveness, Congress appropriated no funding for the Media Campaign in Fiscal Year (FY) 2012, and the campaign is now operating on a minimal budget composed of its unobligated balances as the Youth Drug Prevention Media Program. The Administration has requested $20 million for the Media Program in FY 2013, which will allow the Media Program to implement its two-tiered approach to reach America's young people with anti-drug messaging both at the national level (tier one) and at the community-specific level (tier two).

Mobilize Parents to Educate Youth to Reject Drug Use (1.2.D.) In October 2011, the Department of Defense Education Activity distributed a teacher and parent resource guide in recognition of Red Ribbon Week (October 23rd- 31st) to its 194 schools that serve nearly 85,000 students worldwide. In a collaborative interagency effort with the Drug Enforcement Administration, the Department of Education is revising, updating, and planning to post online one of its most popular publications, *Growing Up Drug-Free: A Parent's Guide to Prevention.*

Develop and Disseminate Information on Youth Drug, Alcohol, and Tobacco Use

Support Substance Abuse Prevention on College Campuses (1.3.A.) In 2011, the Federal Interagency Workgroup on College and University Drinking and Substance Use established a work plan to prevent, address, and manage drinking and substance use on college and university campuses. The Workgroup aims to address underage drinking and drug use as a public health, safety, and economic competitiveness issue requiring the cooperation of all components of campus life. In 2011, the National Institute on Alcohol Abuse and Alcoholism re-convened its College Presidents Working Group, which led a nationwide university and college call to action to prevent underage drinking in 2006. The group works to develop strategies to enhance communication with college and university administrators, reviews newly developed college materials, such as a matrix of best practice approaches to address college drinking, and recommends ideas for research projects for prevention and intervention activities on campuses.

Prepare a Report on Health Risks of Youth Substance Use (1.3.C.) The Office of the Surgeon General completed work on a *Call to Action to Prevent Prescription Drug Abuse among Youth*, scheduled for publication in 2012. This document—the collaborative effort of a Federal interagency workgroup led by the National Institute on Drug Abuse (NIDA)—when completed will contribute to the first objective of the Prescription Drug Abuse Prevention Plan: to raise awareness by educating parents, youth, patients, and health care providers. The Surgeon General's report will describe the scope of the problem and underlying motivations for youth abuse of prescription medications. In addition, the report will recommend specific actions to be taken by various sectors of the community including youth, parents, clinicians, coalitions, law enforcement, and Federal, state, and local agencies.

Criminal Justice Agencies and Prevention Organizations Must Collaborate

Provide Information on Effective Prevention Strategies to Law Enforcement (1.4.A.) Law enforcement agencies are well positioned to promote and participate in community-based drug prevention programs. To assist them in doing so, ONDCP, in collaboration with the Department of Justice and the Department of Health and Human Services, developed an online drug prevention resource. The resource highlights Federally-funded prevention strategies, programs, tools, and resources for law enforcement professionals to support, initiate, facilitate, and lead community-based drug prevention activities. DEA supports numerous community outreach and public education efforts. DEA will continue its current public outreach efforts, expanding the educational presentations, drug information, and teaching tools currently available through its two prevention websites: www.JustThinkTwice.com for teens and www.GetSmartAboutDrugs.com, which is geared towards parents.

Enable Law Enforcement Officers to Participate in Community Prevention Programs in Schools, Community Coalitions, Civic Organizations, and Faith-Based Organizations (1.4.B.) During the past two years, ONDCP provided $5.7 million to the High Intensity Drug Trafficking Areas (HIDTAs) to increase coordination between the law enforcement and prevention communities. Currently, 20 of the 28 HIDTAs fund prevention activities, including all five Southwest Border HIDTA regions. In February 2011, the Department of Homeland Security sponsored a training session on the issues of drug trafficking and its impact on local drug use, counternarcotics data, and border security at the 2011 National Forum of CADCA. A similar training event was conducted in May 2011 to coalitions nationwide via CADCA's web-based training portal. During the 2011 CADCA National Forum, DEA also conducted workshops on marijuana legalization issues and prescription drug abuse. In addition, 86 presentations of PACT360 (Police and Communities Together) were held during 2011, reaching 3,670 individuals. PACT360 is a Department of Justice-funded suite of law enforcement-led drug education programs developed by the Partnership at drugfree.org designed to inform parents and prepare them to address drug-related issues with their teenage children.

Strengthen Prevention Efforts along the Southwest Border (1.4.C.) In 2011, United States Customs and Border Protection, Office of Border Patrol, expanded its Southwest border prevention program, Operation Detour. Operation Detour educates young adults about the dangers and consequences of working for transnational criminal organizations, outlining the ways in which transnational criminal organizations entice young adults into a world of crime. Also in 2011, ONDCP provided outreach training for law enforcement and community leaders in San Diego, California; Tucson, Arizona; and El Paso, Texas. SAMHSA's Collaborative for the Application of Prevention Technologies conducted prevention workforce training in Texas and a series of webinars on sustaining substance use prevention efforts for its grantees in New Mexico. The Indian Health Service's Methamphetamine and Suicide Prevention Initiative funded four programs in and around Tucson and San Diego to provide culturally appropriate interventions, such as the "Keepin' it REAL" program used by the Pascua Yaqui Tribe in Tucson. The U.S. and Mexican governments are also conducting matched studies across the border that will help define the extent of drug use among similar populations and review the impact of Screening, Brief Intervention, and Referral to Treatment services for those populations.

Conclusion

These accomplishments reflect the Administration's belief that preventing drug use before it begins is the most cost-effective, common-sense approach to promoting safe and healthy communities. At the foundation of an effective approach is the recognition that the Nation's drug problems are local and require locally-driven solutions. The Administration is committed to fostering a strong, locally-based prevention infrastructure to ensure that every community is adequately equipped to respond.

Chapter 2. Seek Early Intervention Opportunities in Health Care

Introduction

Early intervention is essential to reducing drug use and its costs to society. Screening, Brief Intervention, and Referral to Treatment (SBIRT) provides an evidence-based approach to early intervention, addressing chronic diseases in medical settings. Research shows that in some instances a brief motivational intervention appears to facilitate abstinence from heroin and cocaine use at a 6-month follow up interview, even in the absence of specialty addiction treatment.[27] SBIRT also reduces the time and resources needed to treat conditions caused or worsened by substance use, making our health systems more cost-effective.[28] For example, participants in the Washington State Screening, Brief Intervention, and Referral to Treatment (WASBIRT) program experienced significant cost savings. Participants that received a brief intervention experienced a reduction in total Medicaid costs ranging from $185-$192 per month. Participants that experienced inpatient hospitalizations from emergency department admissions saw reductions in associated costs ranging from $238-$269 per month. WASBIRT also found a reduction in the number of days of patient hospitalization. Perhaps even more impressive is that, when used with frequently hospitalized patients with chronic conditions, SBIRT reduced future hospital costs related to their care.[29]

Screening for illicit drug use and the use of prescription drugs enables physicians to guard against possible drug interactions and start a conversation about the negative effects of illicit drug use on health. Computer SBIRT holds promise for decreasing several types of illicit drug use in hospitalized women after childbirth.[30] Providing SBIRT in health systems—including primary care, hospitals, and urgent care settings—and ensuring these systems include specialty treatment or referral to treatment brings medical care for substance use disorders into the broader health system as envisioned in the Affordable Care Act.

Accomplishments

Catching Substance Use Disorders Early Saves Lives and Money

Expand and Evaluate Screening for Substance Use in All Health Care Settings (2.1.A.) In 2011, the SAMHSA Center for Substance Abuse Treatment (CSAT) continued to fund 30 SBIRT grantees for substance use disorders. This included nine new awards of 5-year grants to eight states and one territory to expand systems that use SBIRT.[31] In partnership with CSAT, the Health Resources and Services Administration (HRSA) provided technical assistance to grantees seeking guidance with integrating behavioral health into their primary care settings. Further, as part of the technical assistance, a training curriculum was made available for use by health care providers to become proficient in SBIRT.

Reaching Women and Substance-Exposed Infants through Screening and Early Intervention

Use of illicit drugs and alcohol during pregnancy can negatively affect the neurological development and overall health of the baby and can also result in poor maternal health consequences.[32] Each year, an estimated 400,000 infants are affected by prenatal alcohol or illicit drug exposure.[33]

Screening and early intervention in women's healthcare settings has the potential to greatly improve these outcomes. While the American Congress of Obstetricians and Gynecologists recommends substance abuse screening for all women of reproductive age, screening has not been universally adopted, and referrals from screening remain a relatively low proportion of treatment admissions.[34,35]

The Department of Health and Human Services has identified five key intervention points when providers can reach mothers, women, and their families.[36]

1. Pre-Pregnancy—promote awareness of the effects of prenatal substance use, screen, and refer women for appropriate treatment

2. Prenatal—screen and, if needed, refer pregnant women for appropriate treatment as part of routine prenatal care

3. Birth—test newborns for substance exposure at the time of delivery

4. Neonatal—conduct developmental assessments and provide necessary services for the newborn and the family

5. Throughout Childhood and Adolescence—provide ongoing coordinated services for both child and family.

Increase Adoption and Reimbursement of SBIRT Codes (2.1.B.) To insure for SBIRT services, and to further implementation of SBIRT, efforts have been made to encourage states to adopt SBIRT as a reimbursable service with an available set of codes. HRSA has included SBIRT in the Uniform Data Systems to track activity in Federally Qualified Health Center grantees related to substance use disorder screening. SAMHSA has partnered with the Centers for Medicare and Medicaid Services to develop and disseminate the codes available for billing SBIRT services to Medicaid (if adopted by the state) and Medicare to all health care providers in the states. This will help promote the provision of these important screening services.

Integrating SBIRT into Health Care in Colorado

The State of Colorado trains healthcare professionals and clinical support staff through its statewide SAMHSA/CSAT 5-year funding initiative to integrate SBIRT into the standard of care across the state in primary care settings. The funding supports training for Colorado's health care workforce in 22 sites across the State—seven rural clinics (three Federally Qualified Health Centers), one rural hospital, seven urban clinics, six urban hospitals, and one dental clinic. SBIRT provides the tools, counseling, and coaching that healthcare providers and patients in Colorado need to understand the health consequences of substance abuse. Benefits of the practice extend beyond the user—to family, employers, law enforcement, and the healthcare industry. SBIRT Colorado partners with HealthTeamWorks to work with primary care providers throughout the state to integrate the Alcohol and Substance Use Screening Guideline into clinical practice. SBIRT services in Colorado are covered by most insurers with no deductible or co-pays and with no maximums allowed, as defined in the Affordable Care Act. Colorado also supports the integration of SBIRT in non-grant funded sites to include HIV care settings, other Federally Qualified Health Centers, Level I and II trauma centers, the Colorado State Employees Assistance Program, and Multiple Primary Care Physicians utilizing the Colorado SBIRT Clinical Guidelines.

Enhance Health Care Providers' Skills in Screening and Brief Intervention (2.1.C.) Federal agencies that support or operate health care systems have taken the lead in assuring health care professionals are adequately equipped to provide care for individuals with substance use disorders. In 2011, the Department of Health and Human Services, through CSAT, trained 2,279 members in its 17 medical residency programs and other health professionals such as social workers, nurse practitioners, and psychologists on SBIRT implementation. In October 2011, the National Institute on Alcohol Abuse and Alcoholism (NIAAA) released *Alcohol Screening and Brief Intervention for Youth: A Practitioner's Guide*, which will allow medical practitioners to conduct quick and effective screening and brief interventions focused on alcohol use among young people. In 2011, the American Congress of Obstetricians and Gynecologists, in collaboration with CDC, developed the Women and Alcohol website, which offers resources for women's health care providers in identifying women who drink too much and in providing brief educational counseling to reduce or eliminate alcohol use. NIDA is funding a small business grant for the computerized training of primary care providers. The training will be complete in April 2012, and a preliminary evaluation of the program's effectiveness will be available in September 2012.

Conclusion

Medical professionals must be able to identify the early signs of substance use disorders in patients and intervene early. Early interventions in the health care system improve physician awareness of a patient's treatment needs and can result in substantial cost savings to individuals, communities, and the health care system at large. The Administration will continue to promote the integration of SBIRT into mainstream health care, disseminate information about SBIRT to a wide variety of health care settings, highlight model programs that are using SBIRT, and encourage training opportunities for the allied health professions.

Chapter 3. Integrate Treatment for Substance Use Disorders into Health Care and Expand Support for Recovery

Introduction

Integrating substance use disorder treatment into broader health care systems is a high priority for the Administration. Practitioners in mainstream health care systems historically have not screened for substance use disorders and often have limited knowledge of them. As a result, significant resources are spent treating conditions caused or worsened by undiagnosed substance use problems while the quality and cost-effectiveness of substance use disorder treatment is undermined by a failure to identify and address co-occurring medical and mental health conditions. Nonetheless, research has documented that substance use disorder treatment is a sound public investment. For example, a 2006 study found a 7:1 cost offset, meaning that every dollar spent on treatment yielded an average of seven dollars in costs savings. The majority of these savings came from reduced criminal justice system involvement and increased employment earnings.[37] Other studies document substantial cost-offsets in the healthcare domain alone. Another 2006 study reported a net savings of $2,500 per person per year in Medicaid costs associated with treatment, and a State of Washington report found that treatment yielded a con- servatively estimated $252 per person per month in cost reductions associated with medical care and state and community psychiatric hospitalizations.[38,39]

In 2010, an estimated 23.1 million Americans (9.1 percent) aged 12 or older needed specialized treat- ment for a substance use disorder, but only 2.6 million (or roughly 11.2 percent of them) received it. Of those who needed treatment but did not access it, only 5 percent (1.03 million) believed that they needed treatment.[40] This speaks to the need to educate the general public as well as health care prac- titioners on the nature and treatment of substance use disorders and the tools available for supporting sustained recovery. It also highlights the importance of implementing universal screening for substance use problems in primary care and other health care settings and expanding access to treatment and recovery support services.

By requiring that insurers offer coverage for substance use disorder treatment services, the Affordable Care Act will expand access to substance use disorder treatment and help establish it as part of main- stream health care systems. When the Affordable Care Act is fully implemented in 2014, millions more Americans will have coverage. It will therefore be necessary to expand and further train the specialty and primary care workforces. Additionally, substance use disorder treatment providers will need to adopt new business practices, such as ongoing coordination with primary care, the use of electronic health records, and billing Medicaid and private insurance. Similarly, as more Americans gain access to health care coverage, there will be a greater need for substance use disorder screening and addiction-specific services in the primary health care system. Finally, state, local, tribal, and territorial governments will need to adapt their substance use disorder prevention and treatment systems to better integrate them with mainstream health care.

The Administration is focusing its efforts on recovery in three major areas: (1) fostering the development of systems and services that effectively support recovery; (2) increasing public awareness and understanding of addiction and recovery; and (3) eliminating legal and regulatory barriers to recovery.

The Administration is actively working with state, local, and tribal governments to transform systems and services using the Recovery-Oriented Systems of Care (ROSC) framework. The ROSC framework fosters active collaboration and coordination across systems (e.g., specialty addiction, mainstream health care, mental health, child welfare, and criminal justice), emphasizing transparency and shared goals and outcomes. ROSC implementation also relies on the availability of support services mainly delivered by peer-led, faith-based, or other grassroots community organizations. These recovery support services help individuals and families successfully navigate the early months of recovery and provide a flexible and cost-effective mechanism for facilitating access to services and maintaining engagement in them over time. The Administration's efforts to increase public awareness and understanding of addiction and recovery are closely linked with activities to eliminate legal and regulatory barriers to recovery. Addressing laws, rules, and policies that impede efforts at recovery requires awareness of the impact these barriers can have not only on recovering individuals, but on their families, neighborhoods, and communities. The Administration is working to modify or eliminate Federal laws, rules, and policies that prevent recovering individuals from becoming full contributing members of their community.

Accomplishments

Addiction Treatment Must Be an Integrated, Accessible Part of Mainstream Health Care

Expand Addiction Specialty Services in Community Health Centers (3.1.A.) In 2011, HRSA integrated substance use disorder treatment services with primary care in 243 community health centers across the Nation, expanding access to treatment services and eliminating the need for both referral to a specialty provider and the coordination of care across organizations and systems. With full implementation of the Affordable Care Act in 2014, it is anticipated that more community health centers will follow suit, increasing the number of people receiving needed substance use disorder services on-site.

Expand the Innovations of the Department of Veterans Affairs Substance Use Disorder Treatment Approach to Other Federal Health Care Systems (3.1.C.) The Department of Veterans Affairs (VA) and its health services providers have considerable expertise in intervening with and treating substance use disorders among military and veteran populations. To share this expertise with non-VA service providers, as well as service members and veterans themselves, the VA has created a comprehensive online resource center that provides access to screening and assessment tools, VA and Department of Defense clinical practice guidelines, and information on accessing VA treatment services. Also in 2012, the Department of Defense will receive public comments on a proposed rule to lift the prohibition on covering the treatment of substance use disorders through maintenance on substances with addictive potential, such as methadone or buprenorphine. The Department of Defense recognizes that current medical evidence shows that the TRICARE benefit should include such safe and effective treatment options.

Inform Public Health Systems on Implementation of Needle Exchange Programs (3.1.E.) On February 23, 2011, the Department of Health and Human Services published a notice in the Federal Register stating that the Surgeon General of the United States has "determined that a demonstration needle exchange program (or more appropriately called syringe services program or SSP) would be effective in reducing drug abuse and the risk that the public will become infected with the etiologic agent for acquired immune deficiency syndrome."[41] This determination was required by law to permit the expenditure of Substance Abuse Prevention and Treatment Block Grant funds for syringe services programs. Unfortunately, in FY 2012 a Congressional ban was reinstated on most Federal funding for syringe services programs.

Celebrate and Support Recovery from Addiction

Expand the Access to Recovery Program (3.3.A.) In 2010, SAMHSA awarded a new round of funding to 30 Access to Recovery state and tribal grantees. All grantee projects were fully operational by the target date of February 28, 2011, ensuring that programs were quickly able to provide critical services soon after receiving Federal funds. Collectively, the grantees exceeded the target for the number of clients served by nearly 20 percent, serving more than 40,000 persons during the first year of the grant. Additionally, grantees collectively exceeded targets for numbers of participants who abstained from drug use and were not involved with the criminal justice system 6 months after receiving program services.

Review Laws and Regulations that Impede Recovery from Addiction (3.3.B.) Those who have been convicted of certain types of crimes, have completed their sentence, and have made the journey from addiction to recovery are often subject to supplemental sanctions or restrictions for years after their release. Many of these "collateral consequences" of conviction are not exclusive to those who are returning to the community from incarceration—they can also affect individuals who committed a minor drug offense or committed an offense decades in the past and are in stable, long-term recovery. As discussed further in Chapter 4, the Administration, through the Federal Interagency Reentry Council, is working to address barriers to recovery specific to housing, federal student assistance, and collateral consequences of conviction established in state and local laws.

Foster the Expansion of Community-Based Recovery Support Programs, Including Recovery Schools, Peer-Led Programs, Mutual Aid Groups, and Recovery Community Organizations (3.3.C.) In 2010, SAMHSA awarded 11 Targeted Capacity Expansion/Recovery Oriented Systems of Care (TCE/ROSC) grants and five Recovery Community Services Program (RCSP) grants. In 2011, SAMHSA awarded funding to extend the award period for eight RCSP grantees by 6-12 months. The TCE/ROSC program supports coordination of systems and services to effectively support long-term recovery. The RCSP program supports the development of recovery community organizations that provide a wide range of recovery support services. The Administration has convened a Recovery-Oriented Systems of Care (ROSC) learning community, which focuses on planning and implementing the ROSC framework, transforming substance use disorder systems, and sharing effective strategies, policies, protocols, models, or approaches with state, local, tribal, and territorial governments. On September 23, 2011, a joint letter from the Department of Education and ONDCP was sent to officials at colleges and universities throughout the Nation clarifying that recovery support should play an integral role in programs that schools sponsor as part of their legally mandated responsibility to address drug and alcohol problems among their students and staff.

Grassroots Recovery Support in Pennsylvaia

PRO-ACT (Pennsylvania Recovery Organization—Achieving Community Together), a grassroots recovery community organization in Southeastern Pennsylvania, works to reduce the stigma of addiction, ensure the availability of adequate treatment and recovery support services, and inform public opinion and policy regarding the value of recovery. Through its four recovery community centers, PRO-ACT serves an average of 2,400 persons and provides 199 volunteer-run programs, workshops, and training sessions monthly. Through its Ambassadors for Recovery program, PRO-ACT is developing, educating, and mobilizing recovering persons, their family members, friends, and other allies in support of recovery. In 2011, 15,000 persons joined PRO-ACT and other sponsors to march the streets of Philadelphia in support of recovery and take part in a post-march rally as part of PRO-ACT's annual Recovery Month event, *Recovery Walks*! PRO-ACT's three-session Family Education Program brought the tools of recovery to 400 families in 2011 and, since inception, its Mentor+ Program has served 475 inmates in early recovery who were incarcerated for addiction-related crimes, offering them hope, counsel, and support. PRO-ACT is a current Recovery Community Services Program grantee.

ONDCP Director Gill Kerlikowske participates in the presentation of the 2011 National Alcohol and Drug Addiction Recovery Month Proclamation to PRO-ACT Executive Director Beverly Haberle on September 24, 2011.

Conclusion

The Administration has made significant strides in its efforts to integrate substance use disorder services into primary care and support recovery in the community. The Administration will build on these accomplishments in 2012 in order to help more Americans realize the promise of treatment and renewal of recovery.

Chapter 4: Break the Cycle of Drug Use, Crime, Delinquency, and Incarceration

Introduction

The U.S. prison and jail population has reached unacceptable levels. The number of individuals on probation and parole has more than doubled since 1986; over the same period, annual state corrections spending increased from $8 billion to more than $50 billion to keep pace. [42,43,44] In 2010, over seven million people in the United States were under the supervision of the criminal justice system: over two million incarcerated and the remaining five million on probation or parole.[45]

Compounding the significant expenditures on corrections is the fact that far too many offenders return to drug use and reenter the criminal justice system. Among state prisoners with substance use disorders, 53 percent had at least three prior sentences to probation or incarceration, compared to 32 percent of other inmates.[46] Drug dependent or abusing state prisoners (48 percent) were also more likely than other inmates (37 percent) to have been on probation or parole supervision at the time of their arrest.[47] This troubling pattern is due in part to the fact that many offenders deal with a chronic substance use disorder—a disease for which too many are inadequately treated. These offenders need effective substance use disorder and mental health treatment while incarcerated and should continue with recovery support services that assist with employment, housing, medical care, and other support upon their reentry into the community.

The Administration is taking steps to improve the criminal justice system's management of drug-involved offenders exiting the system. Each year, more than 700,000 people are released from state or Federal prison, while another nine million cycle in and out of local jails.[48,49] More than two-thirds of state prisoners are rearrested within 3 years of their release and half are re-incarcerated.[50] Reentry services and support for formerly incarcerated individuals helps to disrupt the cycle of arrest, incarceration, release, and re-arrest. Lifting legal or regulatory barriers is also important to a successful transition to the community.

To reduce these barriers, the Attorney General and the Secretary of Housing and Urban Development issued letters seeking to clarify current policies surrounding former offenders. The Attorney General's letter to state Attorneys General urged them to review the collateral consequences of state laws, such as housing and employment restrictions, that affect ex-offenders leaving the criminal justice system and reentering their communities. As mentioned previously, the Administration is currently leading a similar review of collateral consequences in Federal laws.

In response to widespread misperceptions regarding eligibility for public housing among ex-offenders, the Secretary of Housing and Urban Development's (HUD) letter to executive directors of Public Housing Authorities (PHAs) clarified HUD rules regarding the eligibility of people with criminal records for public housing. In the letter, the Secretary encouraged PHA executive directors "to allow ex-offenders to rejoin their families in the Public Housing or Housing Choice Voucher programs, when appropriate"—an important step in connecting reentering offenders to stable housing and eliminating a significant barrier to recovery.

With the enactment and retroactive application of the Fair Sentencing Act, the disparity in sentencing between offenses for crack cocaine and powder cocaine has been drastically reduced. However, disparities still exist in the justice system—members of minority groups are more likely to be incarcerated for drug offenses and punished with longer sentences than their white counterparts. State prison data show that African American and Hispanic-American individuals who commit drug offenses are consistently incarcerated at higher proportions than white drug offenders—in 2009 alone, there were nearly 66 percent more African Americans in state prison for drug offenses than Caucasians.[51]

The Administration is supporting reform at the Federal level, and states are taking constructive steps through sentencing reform and other criminal justice policy measures, such as drug market interventions, institutional change initiatives, alternatives to incarceration, and evidence-based community supervision and reentry programs, to decrease incarceration rates, reduce recidivism, and control costs.

Accomplishments

Provide Communities with the Capacity to Prevent Drug-Related Crime

Organize Communitywide Efforts to Reduce Open-Air Drug Markets and Gang Activity via Drug Market Intervention Approaches (4.1.A.) The Drug Market Intervention (DMI) model creates clear and predictable sanctions, offers a range of community services, establishes community standards for acceptable behavior, and improves community-police relations through direct engagement among law enforcement, prosecutors, drug dealers and their families, and communities. In 2011, the seven DMI sites funded in Fiscal Year 2010 received training and technical assistance from the Bureau of Justice Assistance (BJA) through its DMI Training and Technical Assistance (TTA) Initiative. BJA also arranged peer to peer exchanges among both established and new DMI sites.[52] The National Institute of Justice (NIJ) is conducting a program evaluation of the DMI TTA Initiative, including an assessment of its impact in the community, which is projected for completion in 2013.

Develop Infrastructure to Promote Alternatives to Incarceration When Appropriate

Support Drug and Other Problem-Solving Courts (4.2.B.) The Administration supports a combined public health and safety approach to addressing substance abusing offenders, and drug courts are a proven part of this approach. They successfully address the substance use disorder and mental health treatment needs of the offender, while still holding them accountable and ensuring public safety. According to the National Association of Drug Court Professionals (www.nadcp.org) there are over 2,600 drug courts currently operating in the United States and they continue to grow. This expansion of drug courts throughout the country makes it critical to ensure that the standards for drug court implementation and operations are effectively disseminated to the field. With funding and technical assistance provided through the National Drug Court Institute, the Administration supports the dissemination of these standards and related training for new and existing courts, as well as the implementation of drug courts in new jurisdictions.

Promote TASC Model of Intensive Case Management (4.2.C.) The National Judicial Leadership Program—Systems Change Initiative, a partnership of CSAT, NIDA, BJA, the National Judicial College, and the Center for Health and Justice at Treatment Alternatives for Safe Communities, trains judges and court leadership on the science of addiction and potential interventions. The Systems Change Initiative held a national judicial training and two state trainings in 2011 for approximately 125 chief or presiding judges and other law enforcement professionals.

2011 Criminal Justice Roundtables

To further advance criminal justice reform, ONDCP Director Gil Kerlikowske held a series of criminal justice policy roundtables focusing on the African American community during the fall of 2011 in Atlanta, Chicago, Los Angeles, New York, and Philadelphia. Director Kerlikowske co-hosted the listening sessions with Congressman John Lewis in Atlanta, Congressman Danny Davis in Chicago, Congresswoman Maxine Waters in Los Angeles, Congressman Ed Towns in New York, and Mayor Michael Nutter in Philadelphia to discuss the Obama Administration's evidence-based approach to reforming the criminal justice system and to hear suggestions on other necessary actions to reduce racial disparities. Attending each session were local African American leaders, judges and law enforcement officials, substance abuse prevention and treatment professionals, community members,

Congressman Danny Davis speaks at a roundtable discussion at Loyola University in Chicago. October 17, 2011

and representatives from national African American organizations. Bringing together a broad swath of local leaders and community members who deal with these issues on a daily basis created an opportunity to discuss the current needs of the community and plan for future collaborative efforts. While each community identified its own specific needs, the roundtables also underscored the common understanding that reducing drug use and its consequences requires a balanced public health and safety approach.

Examine Interventions and Treatment Services for Veterans within the Criminal Justice System (4.2.G.) Veterans Treatment Courts (VTCs) combine rigorous treatment and personal accountability to address the underlying substance use disorder and mental health issues of justice-involved offenders.[53] In addition to the traditional partners in a drug court, VTCs work with veterans agencies and organizations to connect court participants to services for which they are eligible as veterans, including substance use disorder treatment, medical benefits, home loans, and other services provided by the Department of Veterans Affairs that help sustain their long term recovery and reentry to the community.[54] The Administration is taking steps to ensure that the more than 85 VTCs operating today, as well as those in the development stages, operate efficiently and effectively. Funding provided through BJA established the Veterans Treatment Court Planning Initiative, which provides new courts with important standards and best practices. As these courts mature and training continues, the Administration is committed to gathering additional research surrounding their work with justice-involved veterans, as VTCs are showing significant promise in successfully promoting sobriety, recovery, and stability for the Nation's justice-involved veterans.

Connect Incarcerated Veterans with Critical Substance Abuse and Reentry Services (4.2.H.) Working with the Federal Interagency Reentry Council, VA's Veterans Justice Outreach program is clarifying rules regarding health care and benefits eligibility for justice-involved and reentry veterans, ensuring that corrections administrators, service providers, and the veterans themselves understand the implications of incarceration for access to these services, as well as how to reengage them as they reenter society.[55] In addition, DEA and ONDCP are involving military communities and bases in prescription drug safe disposal events, during which service members, veterans, and their families can safely return unused and unwanted medications, preventing those medications from being diverted or misused by others.

Use Community Corrections Programs to Monitor and Support Drug-Involved Offenders

Support Innovative Criminal Justice Research Programs (4.1.C.); Support Drug Testing with Certain and Swift Sanctions in Probation and Parole Systems (4.3.A.) BJA recently funded the Honest Opportunity Probation with Enforcement (HOPE) Field Experiment to test Hawaii's drug testing, random monitoring, and sanctions model for individuals on probation. BJA chose four jurisdictions that vary widely in demographics, population, density, and geographic location—Clackamas County, OR; Essex County, MA; Saline County, AR; and Tarrant County, TX. The National Institute of Justice is conducting a 3.5 year evaluation to determine the impact HOPE has in reducing the number of re-offending probationers, as well as the likely challenges and costs associated with program implementation. NIJ's Multisite Adult Drug Court Evaluation found that adult drug courts significantly reduce drug use and criminal offending—during and after program participation. Participants reported less drug use (56 percent vs. 76 percent) and were less likely to test positive (29 percent vs. 46 percent); and participants reported less criminal activity (40 percent vs. 53 percent) and had fewer re-arrests (52 percent vs. 62 percent, although not a statistically significant difference). Overall, the net benefit of drug courts is an average of $5,680 to $6,208 per participant.[56]

Align the Criminal Justice System and Public Health Systems to Intervene with Heavy Users (4.3.C.) In September 2011, CSAT and BJA announced grant awards for adult drug courts to address public health in the criminal justice system. In FY 2011, CSAT reported an 87.9 percent drug use abstinence rate among clients in drug court grant programs at 6 months post-admission, exceeding its target of 73 percent. Drug court grants served 5,862 clients, which exceeded the target of 5,265 clients.

Tackle Co-Occurring Disorders Using a Community-Based Response (4.3.D.) In 2011, the Administration implemented a number of initiatives aimed at addressing the substance use issues of individuals with co-occurring disorders and other specific needs. CSAT's Treatment for Homeless grants achieved a 164 percent increase in the number of clients being housed, exceeding the target of 50 percent. SAMHSA's Center for Mental Health Services Jail Diversion and Trauma program exceeded its target, with the percentage of clients who had no involvement in the criminal justice system improving from 37.6 percent upon entry to the program to 94 percent at 6 months post-admission, passing the target rate of 92 percent. With regard to drug courts, a new provision was implemented in FY 2011 that requires that all Adult Drug Court requests for application contain language stipulating that grantees must screen for co-occurring disorders.

Create Supportive Communities to Sustain Recovery for the Reentry Population

Expand Reentry Support and Services through Second Chance Act and Other Federal Grants (4.4.A) The Administration's cabinet-level Federal Interagency Reentry Council, led by the Attorney General, coordinates Federal efforts to improve reentry across the Nation. The Council has created an online resource center, including a series of fact sheets called "Reentry Mythbusters," to clarify Federal regulations and policies and address barriers to successful reentry. The resource center contains an interactive calendar listing upcoming trainings and a service directory of state-by-state information.

Develop Ex-Offender Adult Reentry Programs (4.4.B.) The Department of Justice provides grant funding and technical assistance to reentry programs and reentry courts at the state and local level through the Second Chance Act. Successful reentry support programs include services like job placement, drug-free housing, medical care, and substance use disorder and mental health treatment, and other supportive services needed to successfully reenter society and remain out of jail or prison. Reentry courts provide both services and the added guidance of close monitoring.

Facilitate Access to Housing for Reentering Offenders (4.4.C.) Project Reunite engages local public housing authorities to support the successful reunification of formerly incarcerated or chronically homeless men and women with their families. Project Reunite also offers important education and job training to formerly incarcerated individuals to increase employment opportunities. The Administration for Children and Families is providing $6 million to support an integration of the Project Reunite Model into the agency's Healthy Families and Ex-offender Reunification Program, while HUD is simultaneously working to identify private foundations to enhance support from the private sector.

Improve Treatment for Youth Involved with the Juvenile Justice System

Develop and Disseminate More Effective Models of Addressing Substance Abuse and Mental Health Problems among Youth in the Juvenile Justice System (4.5.A.) The Reclaiming Futures initiative, involving SAMHSA, the Office of Juvenile Justice and Delinquency Prevention (OJJDP), and private partnerships, is building the capacity of state, local, tribal, and territorial leaders to establish and improve juvenile drug courts and juvenile court systems to effectively provide treatment for substance use disorders, which is often at the root of so many other problems, including juvenile crime and violence. Through the Second Chance Act, the Administration is expanding mentoring for juvenile offenders during their confinement, transition back to the community, and post-release.

Conclusion

The Administration recognizes the role that the criminal justice system plays in deterring drug use, reducing drug availability, steering users toward the help they need, and making our neighborhoods safer. By recognizing drug addiction as a chronic and progressive disease and working to prevent and treat the underlying substance use disorder, drug related crime and recidivism can be reduced. It makes more sense to support programs and interventions that treat underlying substance use problems rather than to continue to allow individuals with substance use disorders to cycle through the criminal justice system. At all levels of government, fair and effective criminal justice interventions should be combined with evidence-based prevention and treatment efforts to break the cycle of drug use, crime, and incarceration.

Chapter 5. Disrupt Domestic Drug Trafficking and Production

Introduction

Transnational criminal organizations operating in the United States produce, import, or distribute illicit drugs throughout the Nation, posing a persistent and dangerous threat to public health and safety. These organizations use parcel services, tunnels, aircraft, trains, boats, vehicles with hidden compartments, and other conveyances to traffic drugs into and throughout the Nation, particularly along the Southwest and Northern borders. Once in the United States, these organizations increasingly use criminal gangs to control the retail distribution of drugs, particularly in major and midsize cities.[57] In addition to traditional drugs, communities are now concerned with new synthetic drugs, such as those commonly sold as "bath salts" and synthetic cannabinoids sold as "Spice" or "K2". Ultimately, criminal organizations employ complex methods to conceal their illicit profits.

Law enforcement agencies must adjust and adapt to emerging threats and the increasing sophistication of transnational criminal organizations. Domestic law enforcement at the Federal, state, local, tribal, and territorial levels must continue to share information and align resources to identify, disrupt, and dismantle these organizations in the United States. Through the implementation of the *National Southwest Border Counternarcotics Strategy* and the *National Northern Border Counternarcotics Strategy*, the Administration will increase security along the Nation's borders and disrupt and dismantle the transnational criminal organizations that seek to traffic illicit drugs across them.

Accomplishments

Federal Enforcement Initiatives Must be Coordinated with State, Local, and Tribal Partners

Maximize Federal Support for Drug Law Enforcement Task Forces (5.1.A.) During the past two years, Federal law enforcement agencies and their state, local, tribal, and territorial partners have expanded and enhanced drug task forces that are an essential part of reducing drug trafficking and production. In 2011, the rate of participation by state and local law enforcement agencies in Organized Crime Drug Enforcement Task Forces (OCDETF) investigations remained above 90 percent; HIDTA program task forces increased the number of drug trafficking organizations disrupted or dismantled to nearly 3,000 organizations; and DEA offered specialized training to state and local law enforcement agencies while leading 275 task forces nationwide. In a prime example of these coordinated law enforcement efforts, over 300 Federal, state, and local agencies, including OCDETF and HIDTA task forces, as well as foreign agencies, participated in a nationwide takedown coordinated by DEA's Special Operations Division that successfully targeted La Familia Michoacana drug cartel and resulted in over 1,900 arrests and the seizure of approximately $62 million in U.S. currency, $3.8 million in other assets, and thousands of pounds of methamphetamine, cocaine, heroin and marijuana. The trafficking activity had extended into all regions of the United States.

Improve Intelligence Exchange and Information Sharing (5.1.B.) Federal, state, local, tribal, and territorial law enforcement agencies continue to improve intelligence and information sharing through co-location. State and Major Urban Area Fusion Centers are now co-located with eight HIDTA Investigative Support Centers. The newest OCDETF Strike Force, stood up in late 2011, is in the process of co-locating with the HIDTA task force in Chicago, joining numerous other OCDETF Strike Forces that have co-located with HIDTA task forces in their cities. The OCDETF Program launched the OCDETF Fusion Center (OFC) six years ago, and, in the time since, the OFC has become an increasingly important component of U.S. efforts to disrupt and dismantle major criminal organizations, delivering to the field actionable intelligence based upon data sourced from domestic and international agencies. Further, agencies are establishing additional positions at DEA's Special Operations Division and the El Paso Intelligence Center (EPIC) to improve intelligence and information sharing. While these task forces and fusion centers operate nationwide, task force operations also play a vital role along the Nation's borders. The 24 Integrated Border Enforcement Teams on the Northern border and 29 operational Border Enforcement Security Task Forces in the United States and Mexico illustrate cooperative efforts among Federal, state, local, tribal, and international counterparts. Federal law enforcement agencies continue to participate in intelligence-driven operations with tribal law enforcement agencies along the Nation's borders. For example, in October 2011, a U.S. Immigration and Customs Enforcement (ICE) Homeland Security Investigations (HSI) Shadow Wolves patrol unit working with the Tohono O'odham Nation Police Department seized nearly two tons of marijuana on tribal lands.

Ensure Comprehensive Review of Domestic Drug Threat (5.1.F.) Federal agencies continue to refine their understanding of the drug trade, drug use, and their impact. With the closure of the National Drug Intelligence Center at the end of Fiscal Year 2012, the Federal Government must identify alternative sources for comprehensive, domestic, strategic analysis. ONDCP will work with Federal agencies, including DOJ, DHS, and the Office of the Director of National Intelligence to ensure that law enforcement, intelligence, and interdiction agencies are able to harness their individual authorities, sources of information, and analytic abilities cooperatively to provide the President, ONDCP, and other national policymakers with the information essential for establishing sound policies to curtail drug use and its consequences.

U.S. Borders Must be Secured

Implement the Southwest Border Counternarcotics Strategy (5.2.A.) The Administration has deployed unprecedented technology, personnel, and resources along the Southwest border. From FY 2009- 2011, the Department of Homeland Security has seized 41 percent more drugs, 74 percent more currency, and 159 percent more weapons along the Southwest border as compared to FY 2006-2008. The Border Patrol increased its agents from approximately 10,000 in 2004 to more than 21,000 today, with nearly 18,500 agents stationed along the Southwest border. The Federal Bureau of Investigation (FBI) established its Latin American Southwest Border Section, strengthening intelligence-driven investigations targeting transnational criminal organizations impacting the Southwest border. Additionally, DEA has allocated nearly 28 percent of its domestic agent positions to the Southwest border, and HSI has deployed a quarter of its operational personnel to the region. The Department of Justice has also secured a dramatically higher number of extraditions from Mexico (93 in 2011, compared to 12 in 2000) and has trained over 5,400 Mexican prosecutors and investigators.

Develop National Plan for Southbound Interdiction of Currency and Weapons (5.2.C.) To enhance efforts to combat bulk cash smuggling, ICE expanded its operations at the Bulk Cash Smuggling Center in 2011. Established in 2009, the Bulk Cash Smuggling Center is a 24/7 investigative support and operations center designed to assist ICE and its international and domestic law enforcement partners with the investigation, seizure, forfeiture, and arrest of subjects involved in transnational crimes that are facilitated by the movement of illicit proceeds through bulk cash smuggling. Since its inception, the center has initiated over 450 criminal investigations, which have resulted in nearly 270 criminal arrests and the seizure of more than $170 million.

Coordinate Efforts to Secure the Northern Border against Drug-Related Threats (5.2.D.) The Administration also developed the first *National Northern Border Counternarcotics Strategy*, building upon existing architecture, identifying needed resources, and enlisting state, local, and tribal law enforcement in a genuine partnership under the framework of the Beyond the Border initiative the United States has undertaken with Canada. In order to develop the *National Northern Border Counternarcotics Strategy*, the Administration consulted with Canadian, Federal, state, local, and tribal government agencies and conducted a series of roundtable discussions across the Northern border. In August 2011, NDIC finalized the *Northern Border Drug Threat Assessment*, a strategic assessment addressing the current and emerging threats associated with drug trafficking and related criminal activities on the U.S.-Canada border.

Developing the *National Northern Border Counternarcotics Strategy*

Ben Tucker, ONDCP Deputy Director for State, Local, and Tribal Affairs, visits the U.S.-Canada border during ONDCP's 2011 consultation tour.

The *National Northern Border Counternarcotics Strategy* is the product of an extensive consultation process that began with hundreds of letters soliciting input from relevant Congressional delegations and Federal, state, local, and tribal law enforcement officials. To enhance this consultation process, Administration officials conducted a five-state consultation tour that included stops in Seattle, Washington; Blackfeet Nation, Montana; Grand Forks, North Dakota; Detroit, Michigan; and upstate New York. The consultation meetings included discussions with the U.S. Attorneys, the HIDTA Directors, and panels of Federal, state, local, and tribal officials. At each location, law enforcement officials highlighted successes and provided recommendations to strengthen our efforts to secure the Northern border against drug trafficking and related threats.

Deny Use of Ports of Entry and Routes of Ingress and Egress Between the Ports (5.2.E.) U.S. Customs and Border Protection continues to expand capacity and cooperation with international partners to stem the flow of drugs and disrupt transnational criminal organizations through enforcement operations at the ports of entry. For example, working with Mexico and Canada, the Next Generation of Integrated Cross-Border Law Enforcement (NxtGen) pilot mission involves a multitude of entities working together in a seamless and integrated way. The tenets of NxtGen are to deter and prevent terrorism and transnational threats at the earliest opportunity; detect and prevent illegal entry and other illegal cross-border activity; expedite the efficient flow of lawful trade and travel within North America; and ensure the two nations' (United States and Canada) shared communities, critical infrastructure, and populations are mutually prepared and protected through bi-national and bilateral security, resilience, and response protocols and activities.

Focus National Efforts on Specific Drug Problems

Counter Domestic Methamphetamine Production (5.3.A.) The Administration remains committed to reducing the production, trafficking, and use of methamphetamine. In Calendar Year 2011, 6,197 methamphetamine laboratories were seized nationwide, according to the DEA National Seizure System. The total number of laboratories seized nationwide was approximately 24.5 percent higher than in 2010. While the numbers of total laboratory seizures continues to climb, the laboratories seized are smaller and produce significantly smaller quantities. Nevertheless, the danger posed by the smaller labs remains significant. Several options are being considered to further reduce methamphetamine production, including prescription-only status for pseudoephedrine/ephedrine products. Improved restrictions that are designed to eliminate smurfing would decrease the number of methamphetamine laboratories and the corresponding dangers they pose. DEA continues to dedicate enforcement, intelligence, and other resources to prevent the diversion of pseudoephedrine/ephedrine products to the manufacture of methamphetamine, and to disrupt the abuse, trafficking, and transportation of methamphetamine, to include providing state and local law enforcement officers with training related to clandestine laboratories and methamphetamine production.

Eradicate Marijuana Cultivation (5.3.C.) Violent transnational criminal organizations exploit public and tribal lands as grow sites for marijuana. In 2011, Operation Full Court Press used tested enforcement strategies to reduce marijuana cultivation on public lands in California. Operation Full Court Press was a three week long, multi-agency marijuana operation in Colusa, Glenn, Lake, Mendocino, Tehama, and Trinity counties. Targeting large-scale illegal marijuana grow operations in and around the Mendocino National Forest, the operation consisted of more than 300 personnel from 25 Federal, state, and local agencies, resulting in the seizure of 632,058 marijuana plants and the arrest of 159 individuals. Further, through the Public Lands Drug Coordination Committee, Federal agencies are coordinating policies and programs to support field-level eradication operations, investigations, and intelligence and information sharing.

Conclusion

This past year also saw a number of emerging challenges, to include the rising threat of synthetic cathinones marketed as "bath salts" and synthetic cannabinoids marketed as "herbal incense." According to the 2011 Monitoring the Future Survey, one in nine high school seniors had used "Spice" or "K2" (products containing synthetic cannabinoids) during the past year, which makes synthetic cannabinoids the second most frequently used illicit drug, after marijuana, among high school seniors.[58] DEA used its emergency scheduling authority to temporarily control five synthetic cannabinoids that were commonly laced on products marketed as "herbal incense" and three synthetic cathinones that were commonly found in products marketed as "bath salts." The Administration is also encouraging states to enact measures to control these substances to ensure that state law enforcement agencies have the authority to investigate production, trafficking, and sales of these dangerous products. As of December 2011, 33 states had enacted laws to control "bath salts" (synthetic cathinones), while 43 states had adopted laws to ban chemical substances related to synthetic cannabinoids.[59,60] Law enforcement agencies have adapted their investigative tools to target these emerging threats. For example, the DEA New York Field Division established a Bath Salts Task Force to investigate sellers of the drug in the greater New York City area. In June 2011 the task force arrested a major distributor of "bath salts" and nine employees of retail shops that sold the drug. In December 2011 the House of Representatives passed legislation that would ban synthetic drugs, and the Administration will continue to work with Congress throughout 2012 to address the emerging threat of synthetic drugs.

Close collaboration and leveraging resources among Federal, state, local, tribal, and territorial law enforcement, community coalitions, and other stakeholders is more critical than ever. Through working together and effectively drawing upon the strengths of stakeholders, communities can effect change and respond to the drug threat.

Chapter 6: Strengthen International Partnerships

Introduction

International drug control cooperation is focused on reducing the supply of illicit drugs in the United States while assisting nations that are adversely affected by the illicit drug trade. By embracing the concept of "shared responsibility" and engaging in effective cooperation, the United States—working with international partners—can reduce illicit drug use, production, trafficking, and associated violence. Reductions in supply are often closely tied to reductions in drug use and its consequences.

The cooperative effort between the United States and Colombia to disrupt the cocaine market is a case in point. During the past decade, the United States and Colombia have worked together to reduce drug production, strengthen the rule of law, and increase citizen security that had been threatened by drug-funded terrorist and criminal organizations. As a result, potential production capacity for pure cocaine in Colombia was reduced from an estimated 700 metric tons in 2001 to 270 metric tons in 2010, a 61 percent decline.[61,62,63] This unprecedented reduction in cocaine availability has been accompanied by

- lower rates of cocaine use in the United States as reported in surveys of both adults and young people;

- significant declines in the number of arrestees testing positive for cocaine in many U.S. cities; and

- historic reductions in the rates of adults testing positive for cocaine in the workplace.[64,65,66]

The Administration's international counternarcotics programs are ultimately designed to reduce drug production and trafficking, promote alternative livelihoods, and strengthen rule of law, democratic institutions, citizen security, and respect for human rights. Countries facing the threats of drug production and trafficking often also experience increasing rates of drug use. The Administration's international programs promote effective demand reduction interventions, to include building institutions to provide alternatives to incarceration, healthy alternatives for at-risk youth, improved drug treatment capacities, and programs that help build strong and resilient communities.

International drug control partnerships protect public health and safety, while contributing to overall national security. The success of these international efforts is highly influenced by the commitment and cooperation of governments, international institutions, and civil society organizations that provide drug-related assistance around the globe. The Administration will continue to prioritize international programs with a focus on those regions most important to reducing drug availability, drug use, and their consequences in the United States.

Accomplishments

Collaborate with International Partners to Disrupt the Drug Trade

Conduct Joint Counterdrug Operations with International Partners (6.1.A.) DEA continues to work with international partners in 65 countries to target the most significant illicit drug and chemical trafficking organizations in the world. In FY 2011, DEA trained 2,769 international law enforcement professionals; opened two new DEA offices in Portugal and Indonesia; and conducted Operation All-Inclusive in the Western Hemisphere, an interagency and international operation that targets the flow of drugs, money, and precursor chemicals from the source zone through the transit zone and into the United States. Also in 2011, the United States Coast Guard sponsored the Multilateral Maritime Counter Drug Summit (MMCDS). The semi-annual MMCDS provides participating nations an opportunity to share and exchange "best practices" and to employ new tactics, techniques, and procedures to combat transnational criminal organizations. Participating nations in the 2011 MMCDS included Belize, Colombia, Costa Rica, Ecuador, Guatemala, Mexico, Nicaragua, Panama, Peru, and the United States.

Work with Partner Nations and OAS/CICAD to Strengthen Counterdrug Institutions in the Western Hemisphere (6.1.B.) In the fall of 2010 the United States was elected to a 2-year term as chair of the Organization of American States/Inter-American Drug Abuse Control Commission (OAS/CICAD) Demand Reduction Experts Group. Under the U.S. chairmanship, the Experts Group embarked on a program to produce model guidance for the nations of the hemisphere on four key issues: community-based prevention, drugged driving, prescription drug abuse, and demand-related data collection. The community-based prevention initiative will culminate in the development of guidelines for community participation in programs for drug prevention, treatment, and recovery, emphasizing collaboration among law enforcement, the judiciary, non-governmental organizations, civil society, and multiple levels of government.

Work with Partners in Europe, Africa, and Asia to Disrupt Drug Flows in the Trans-Atlantic and Trans-Pacific Regions (6.1.C.) Transnational criminal organizations take advantage of limited law enforcement capacities in West African nations to traffic illegal drugs from the Western Hemisphere to markets in Europe and beyond. The Department of State and the European Union brought together over 300 senior law enforcement and judicial officials from 65 countries on both sides of the Atlantic at the Trans-Atlantic Symposium to Dismantle Transnational Illicit Networks in May 2011 to devise strategies and identify initiatives to combat trans-Atlantic organized crime activities, including narcotics trafficking. Through its West Africa Cooperative Security Initiative, the U.S. Government supports the governments of West Africa in their efforts to address the facilitating factors and the corrosive and debilitating effects of transnational organized crime in the region. In one example of ongoing cooperation with African nations, the Coast Guard Cutter FORWARD participated in the 2011 Africa Maritime Law Enforcement Partnership, conducting combined maritime patrols with Sierra Leone, Senegal, and Cape Verde. The Department of Homeland Security is also cultivating partnerships in this area of the world, with several joint initiatives involving the United Kingdom and Nigeria's customs and immigration agencies. Information on individual smugglers, international smuggling routes and patterns, and specifics of cartel involvement is collected and shared among the respective agencies for effective interception upon arrival in each country.

Coordinate with Global Partners to Prevent Synthetic Drug Production and Precursor Chemical Diversion (6.1.D.) Global efforts to prevent the diversion of precursor chemicals are complex, requiring cooperation with governments, multilateral organizations, and the private sector. In 2010, the UN Commission on Narcotic Drugs voted in favor of tightening controls on phenylacetic acid, a methamphetamine precursor chemical. A number of countries also approved legislation to monitor imports and exports of ephedrine and pseudoephedrine—non-controlled precursor chemicals used to produce methamphetamine. The Department of Defense, through the Hawaii-based Joint Interagency Task Force West, is contributing to the global precursor chemical control effort through the analysis of precursor and methamphetamine production and trafficking trends and through the exchange of information with countries in the region. In addition to cooperation on methamphetamine-related precursor chemicals, the United States is also working with our international partners to address production and trafficking of other precursors including acetic anhydride and potassium permanganate, as well as synthetic cannabinoids and synthetic cathinones.

Expand Global Prevention and Treatment Initiatives Bilaterally and Through Cooperation with the United Nations, the Organization of American States, the Colombo Plan, and Other Multilateral Organizations (6.1.E.) At the 2011 meeting of the United Nations Commission on Narcotics Drugs (CND), the United States promoted innovative criminal justice programs (such as those discussed in Chapter 4) that employ testing and sanctions for drug involved offenders. As follow-up to a U.S.-sponsored CND resolution, ONDCP, the Canadian Centre on Substance Abuse, and the European Monitoring Centre for Drugs and Drug Addiction sponsored the first International Symposium on Drugs and Driving, held in Montreal, Canada in July 2011. In the Western Hemisphere, the United States has exercised leadership through OAS/CICAD, most recently as the Chair of the Demand Reduction Experts Group mentioned previously. In Afghanistan, in collaboration with the Colombo Plan, the United States has facilitated the development of over 30 drug treatment centers serving over 10,000 individuals with substance use disorders, including six specialized centers for women and children and three for adolescents.

Enhance the Relationship Developed with Russia under the U.S.-Russia Bilateral Presidential Commission (6.1.G.) The U.S. Director of National Drug Control Policy and the Director of the Russian Federal Drug Control Service serve as the co-chairs of the Counternarcotics Working Group (CNWG) of the U.S.-Russia Bilateral Presidential Commission, leading an effort to improve cooperation in the three key areas of drug demand reduction, countering illicit finance, and drug law enforcement operations. Since the creation of the CNWG, U.S. and Russian law enforcement authorities have conducted cooperative enforcement operations and engaged in numerous joint training activities. The United States and Russia have also engaged in extensive exchanges on initiatives that effectively reduce the demand for drugs, including visits by Russian authorities to prevention, treatment, and recovery agencies and programs in Los Angeles, Baltimore, Chicago, and the Washington, D.C. area. These exchanges have yielded results, including an effort by the Russian Government to establish alternatives to incarceration for minor or first time offenders, offering treatment in lieu of jail time when appropriate.

Support the Drug Control Efforts of Major Drug Source and Transit Countries

Strengthen Strategic Partnerships with Mexico (6.2.A.) The Merida Initiative is a cooperative response to organized crime by the United States and the Government of Mexico, with the ultimate goal of breaking the power and impunity of transnational criminal organizations, thus increasing public security and safety. The United States and Mexico acknowledge shared responsibilities to counter the drug-fueled violence that threatens citizens in both countries. Through the Merida Initiative, the United States is providing the Mexican law enforcement community with technical assistance, training, and mentorship. The United States is also providing assistance to the Mexican judiciary in an effort to support an increase in prosecutorial capacity building, judicial and prison reform, justice sector institution building, information technology enhancement, infrastructure development, and border security. The Merida Initiative has wide bipartisan support in Congress, which has appropriated a total of $1.9 billion under the initiative. The Twenty-First Century Border Management declaration, issued by Presidents Obama and Calderon in May 2010, has provided a framework for increased bilateral efforts at the border, to include efforts to facilitate legitimate trade and travel and better address violence and criminality. Additionally, the North American Maritime Security Initiative (NAMSI) between the United States, Mexico, and Canada facilitates successful trilateral counterdrug operations in the maritime domain.

Disrupt the Narcotics-Insurgency Nexus and the Narcotics-Corruption Nexus in Afghanistan (6.2.B.) As the United States draws down combat forces and transitions U.S.-supported programs, enabling Afghanistan to establish capable and credible counternarcotics forces remains critical. As an example of growing counternarcotics capacity, Afghan-led coalition forces executed 521 narcotics interdiction operations in 2011. These operations included partnered patrols, cordon-and-search actions, detentions, and overwatch operations. They resulted in 644 arrests and led to the seizure of 152,997 kg of hashish, 65,537 kg of opium, 21,275 kg of morphine, 7,045 kg of heroin, and 139,349 kg of narcotics-related chemicals.[67]

Build the Law Enforcement and Criminal Justice Capacities of Source Countries in the Western Hemisphere to Sustain Progress against Illicit Drug Production and Trafficking (6.2.C.) In March 2011, President Obama announced the Central America Citizen Security Partnership, which works with governments to expand law enforcement, judicial, social, and educational capacities and services to counter the activities and influence of organized crime in the region. The Merida Initiative is also supporting this action: over 4,300 Federal Police have already completed training at Mexico's Federal Police Academy in San Luis Potosí with the assistance of U.S. funding. In collaboration with the Colombian Ministry of Defense, the Colombian Military has established a pilot training program for Mexican helicopter aviators, and the Colombian National Police has conducted two 8-week Rural Operations Courses and an eight-week Paramedic course. FBI has been supporting Mexico through extensive international law enforcement training and investigative support, including through its Resolution 6 and Legal Attaché programs. U.S. assistance has helped Mexican police and customs officials expand and improve canine teams used in the interdiction of narcotics, firearms, explosives, and other contraband.

Implement the Caribbean Basin Security Initiative (6.2.D.) The Caribbean Basin Security Initiative (CBSI) further strengthens the key institutions of our Caribbean partners to face the challenges of transnational crime and reduced economic opportunities. The United States is working with partner nations to promote community-based policing and demand-reduction and anti-gang efforts. CBSI is a regional initiative and a pillar of the U.S. security strategy focused on citizen safety throughout the hemisphere. It is focused on three core objectives to deal with the threats facing the Caribbean: reduce illicit trafficking, advance public safety and security, and promote social justice. In addition to assisting our foreign partners in the region under CBSI, the Administration is also committed to working with the Commonwealth of Puerto Rico and the U.S. Virgin Islands to address drug-related public safety challenges, focusing on strengthening the justice sector and providing greater opportunities for young people.

Promote Alternative Livelihoods for Coca and Opium Farmers (6.2.E.) Promoting alternative livelihoods, particularly when combined with increased government presence and clear deterrents to illicit crop cultivation (eradication or the threat of eradication), has effectively reduced illicit crop cultivation in targeted areas. For example, in Peru's San Martin region, the eradication and alternative development components have worked together effectively to dramatically reduce coca cultivation. The Department of State's Narcotics Affairs Section has effectively sponsored consistent manual eradication efforts in San Martin, resulting in a dramatic reduction of illicit coca cultivation to insignificant levels. Peru, with USAID support, has cultivated thousands of hectares of sustainable economic alternatives such as cacao, coffee, and oil palm trees, without which communities would again be vulnerable to narco-trafficking influence.[68]

Support the Central American Regional Security Initiative (6.2.F.) The United States is working with its partners to address citizen security in Central America by reducing the involvement of criminal organizations in destabilizing governments, threatening national security and public safety, and by preventing the trafficking of drugs to countries throughout the region and the United States. Key to this initiative will be greater political and resource commitment among the governments of the region, increased donor coordination, and more focused, accelerated, and coordinated U.S. assistance.

Leverage Capacities of Partner Nations and International Organizations to Help Coordinate Programs in the Western Hemisphere (6.2.G.) The Administration is strengthening international drug control partnerships in the Western Hemisphere in pursuit of four main objectives: disrupt and dismantle transnational criminal organizations that derive significant amounts of income from drug trafficking; reduce illicit drug consumption; reduce illicit drug supply; and strengthen the capacity of democratic institutions to address the consequences of illicit drugs. Congress has appropriated $1.64 billion for the Merida Initiative for Mexico through FY 2011, and nearly $900 million worth of equipment and assistance had been delivered through calendar year 2011. Through FY 2011, the Central America Regional Security Initiative was supported with a total of $361.508 million and the Caribbean Basin Security Initiative was supported with $139.124 million. Funding levels for these programs for FY 2012 are currently being determined in consultation with Congress, pursuant to U.S. law. For FY 2013 the Administration has requested $234 million for Merida/Mexico, $107.5 million for CARSI, and $59 million for CBSI.

Consolidate the Gains Made in Colombia (6.2.H.) The United States continues to support Colombia's National Consolidation Plan while the Government of Colombia develops the independent capacity to address drug trafficking and ensure the consolidation of the counternarcotics gains made under Plan Colombia. Colombia plays a leading role in the hemisphere, sharing its vast counternarcotics experience to assist others in reducing illicit drug trafficking and consumption and increasing law enforcement capacity to improve citizen security. While cocaine production potential in Colombia decreased between 2001 and 2010, production potential elsewhere has held steady or gradually increased in recent years. Coca cultivation in Peru increased by 33 percent between 2009 and 2010, and for the first time in recent history potential pure Peruvian cocaine production exceeded that of Colombia.[69] The expulsion of DEA by the Government of Bolivia is a serious obstacle in Bolivia's efforts to confront transnational criminal organizations involved in drug trafficking. Bolivia has yet to reverse the increases in net coca cultivation of the past several years, although in 2010 it appeared that production had stabilized. However, without the ability to conduct yield studies previously conducted by the DEA, there is no assurance that production has not risen. Despite these challenges, the United States remains committed to working in partnership with national governments to counter drug production and trafficking in the Andean region.

Attack Key Vulnerabilities of Drug Trafficking Organizations

Disrupt Illicit Drug Trafficking in the Transit Zone (6.3.B.) For over two decades, the U.S. interagency law enforcement, intelligence, and military team, coordinated through JIATF South, has worked together with partner nations to stem the flow of illicit drugs through the Western Hemisphere. The Panama Express Program (PANEX), a multi-agency task force dedicated to disrupting and dismantling major maritime drug transport organizations based in South and Central America, has contributed to the interdiction of over 850 tons of cocaine in international waters destined for the United States or its Southern neighbors. PANEX has resulted in over 2,100 individuals being brought to the United States for prosecution—with a 97 percent conviction rate. The Administration has maintained a national goal to remove 40 percent of documented cocaine movement through the transit zone by the year 2015. This goal has been pursued through increasing annual removal targets, starting with a 25 percent removal target in 2008. Unlike in 2010, in 2011, the removal rate fell short of the annual target. Total removals of 193 metric tons, divided by total documented movement, yielded a removal rate of 25 percent—short of the 32 percent target for the year. A multitude of factors influence interdiction success achieved in any given year, but increasingly limited resources for detection, monitoring, and interdiction played a major role in the 2011 shortfall. Increasing and improving collaboration with U.S. partner nations and allied counterparts is of continuing importance.

Target the Illicit Finances of Drug-Trafficking Organizations (6.3.C.) Law enforcement efforts are focusing on bulk cash smuggling, money laundering, asset seizure and forfeiture, and the protection of legitimate economic systems and institutions. In FY 2011, DEA seized a total of $745,530,240 from drug trafficking and money laundering organizations. FBI's seizures and forfeitures related to drug trafficking organizations amounted to $51,578,721 in FY 2011. Also in 2011, the HSI National Bulk Cash Smuggling Center (BCSC) assumed control of the EPIC Bulk Cash Unit (EBCU) and Analysis Section, which will improve the sharing of bulk cash interdiction and seizure information to support law enforcement operations.

The Joint Interagency Task Forces (JIATF)—International Cooperation Yielding Results

JIATF South: International Cooperation Leads to Aircraft Interdiction in Honduras

JIATF South employs a "defense forward" strategy to detect, monitor, and interdict illicit trafficking events in the Western Hemisphere. The suspect aircraft pictured here was initially detected by Colombian ground-based radar, U.S. radar systems, and U.S. Air Force aircraft. JIATF South coordinated the launch of a Colombian Air Force jet, which visually identified and tracked the suspect aircraft into Honduras. JIATF South also coordinated the launch of a Honduran Air Force jet as well as the launch of two helicopters carrying DEA agents and a Honduran Tactical Response Team. When the suspect aircraft landed, the Colombian Air Force crew observed the traffickers as they trans-ferred the contraband into trucks and then set fire to the empty

Cocaine traffickers had set fire to their aircraft shortly before being apprehended by law enforcement authorities in Honduras in August 2011.

aircraft. The helicopters followed the trucks until they stopped and then deployed the Honduran Tactical Response Team to interdict the load and apprehend the traffickers, resulting in the seizure of 470 kilograms of cocaine.

JIATF West: Attacking the Precursor Supply Chain

Joint Interagency Task Force West (JIATF West) focuses on tracking and interdicting Asia-sourced precursor chemicals that are used to produce methamphetamine. Since 2010, tracking and interdiction efforts have resulted in the seizure of up to 900 metric tons of illicit Asian-sourced precursor chemicals, preventing the production of 180 metric tons of methamphetamine. Diminished access to precursor chemicals has finan-cially impacted and weakened transnational criminal organizations that smuggle precursor chemicals from China and India for use in methamphetamine production in Mexico. Ongoing interdiction efforts have caused traffickers to shift precursor shipments to Central and South America, use less efficient production methods, and rely on less desirable substitute chemicals.

Target Cartel Leadership (6.3.D.) Throughout FY 2011, U.S. law enforcement agencies continued to target the most wanted drug trafficking and money laundering organizations believed to be primar-ily responsible for the Nation's illicit drug supply. OCDETF coordinates the annual formulation of the Consolidated Priority Organization Target (CPOT) List, a multi-agency target list of "command and con-trol" elements of the most significant international drug trafficking and money laundering organizations. From the implementation of the CPOT list in June 2002 through FY 2011, 29 CPOT organizations have been disrupted and 49 dismantled, six of which were dismantled during FY 2011. Additionally, during FY 2011 the Department of Treasury's Office of Foreign Assets Control designated four CPOTs and their financial and commercial networks for targeted financial sanctions.

Conclusion

Moving forward, the Administration remains committed to reducing the flow of drugs into the United States while also combating other related forms of transnational organized crime. On July 25, 2011, the Administration released the *Strategy to Combat Transnational Organized Crime*, the first whole-of-government strategy to address this dynamic threat in more than a decade. In the time since the *Strategy's* release, the Administration has moved forward with the implementation of a number of its most important components, including an Executive Order to block the property of and prohibit transactions with significant transnational criminal networks; a legislative package that will enhance the authorities available to investigate, interdict, and prosecute the activities of top transnational criminal networks; a Presidential Proclamation that will deny transnational criminal aliens entry to the United States; and a rewards program that will help obtain information leading to the arrest and conviction of the leaders of transnational criminal organizations. In support of the *Strategy*, in December 2011, the U.S. Senate passed the Transnational Drug Trafficking Act of 2011, an important piece of legislation that will strengthen U.S. efforts to prosecute illicit drug traffickers who operate beyond our borders.

Chapter 7. Improve Information Systems for Analysis, Assessment, and Local Management

Introduction

The Administration has repeatedly emphasized the principle that policy must be based upon sound scientific evidence—a principle that is particularly relevant to drug policy. The *National Drug Control Strategy* promotes drug prevention, treatment, and law enforcement policies and programs that are evidence-based and proven to be effective.

When formulating drug policy—be it the *Prescription Drug Abuse Prevention Plan*, the drugged driving initiative, the *National Southwest Border Counternarcotics Strategy*, or any other policy—one of the first steps is to identify the scope of the problem to be addressed. Accurate and timely data are required to fully understand the various aspects of the issue, including the populations affected, the prevalence of the drug use problem, the latest drug trafficking patterns, and the trends in the behavior of interest (e.g., are opioid prescription drug overdose deaths increasing?)

Once a policy or program is formulated and implemented, accurate and timely data are required to help manage the policy or program—especially at the local level, where most programs are implemented—and to assess the fidelity of program delivery and effectiveness. The routine and systematic collection of data on how a policy or program is administered helps policymakers determine whether improvements in implementation are required over time. Ideally, rigorous outcome evaluations should be developed to provide data on whether the policy or program is effective at achieving its stated goals and objectives.

Information systems need to be continually maintained and monitored for quality, and improvements need to be made in accordance with methodological advancements. Estimates of critical indicators based upon data generated by these systems can be negatively affected by methodological limitations and drops in the rigor with which the systems are implemented, which, in turn, can result in the use of inaccurate information in the policymaking process.

Accomplishments

The Administration's first *National Drug Control Strategy* presented a coordinated plan for improving information systems so that the required data are available for the formulation and assessment of drug policy and programs. In developing this plan, there were three guiding principles: (1) existing Federal data systems need to be sustained and enhanced; (2) new data systems and analytical methods to address gaps should be developed and implemented; and (3) measures of drug use and related problems must be useful at the state and community level. In the time since the release of the first Strategy, there have been significant accomplishments in improving our understanding of drug trends and in increasing the speed of our policy responses.

Existing Federal Data Systems Need to Be Sustained and Enhanced

Several existing Federal data systems that provide critical information on drug use, consequences, or supply are in need of improvements or are facing resource challenges. To ensure that the *Strategy* formulation, implementation, and assessment process is kept sufficiently informed by the most accurate and timely data, these systems must be improved and adequately resourced.

Enhance the Drug Abuse Warning Network System (DAWN) (7.1.A.) DAWN is a public health surveillance system that monitors drug-related hospital emergency department visits to track the impact of drug use, misuse, and abuse in the United States. These data provide policymakers with situational awareness regarding trends in the morbidity of illicit drug use. DAWN is being phased out, to be replaced by the enhancement of the ambulatory component of a CDC survey (the National Hospital Care Survey). This survey will collect similar data on drug-related visits to emergency departments. The data will be collected at lower costs and provide more information on patient outcomes. SAMHSA has transferred funds to CDC to begin a pilot study; data from the new system will be available in 2013.

Improve the National Survey on Drug Use and Health (NSDUH) (7.1.B.) NSDUH is an annual nationwide survey that collects data on the levels and patterns of substance use. Data from NSDUH provide representative national and state-level estimates on the use of tobacco products, alcohol, and illicit drugs (including non-medical use of prescription drugs) in the United States. These data provide the drug prevention, treatment, and research communities with current, relevant information on the nature of drug and alcohol use and the consequences of abuse. SAMHSA is redesigning NSDUH for full implementation in 2014-2015. Initial steps are already underway, such as gathering recommendations from Federal agencies and various user groups for improvement (e.g., obtaining data on people in recovery). In particular, the new design will incorporate recent changes in prescription drug product type and availability. Recommendations and supporting materials will be posted for public review and comment.

Sustain Support for the Drug and Alcohol Services Information System (DASIS) (7.1.C.) DASIS is the primary source of national information on the services available for substance abuse treatment and the characteristics of individuals admitted to treatment. DASIS contains three data sets that are maintained with the cooperation and support of the states: 1) the Inventory of Substance Abuse Treatment Services (I-SATS), an electronic master list of all organized substance abuse treatment facilities known to SAMHSA, 2) the National Survey of Substance Abuse Treatment Services (N-SSATS), an annual survey of the treatment providers on the I-SATS; and 3) the Treatment Episode Data Set (TEDS), a national database containing a minimum data set of information about admissions to treatment (primarily by providers receiving public funding). SAMHSA is currently implementing a plan to ensure the continued viability of DASIS so states will continue to be able to provide comprehensive and timely data on treatment admissions to specialty facilities.

Better Assess Price and Purity of Illicit Drugs on the Street (7.1.D.) DEA is investigating the expansion of heroin purchase collection in the Midwest to improve the resolution of source signatures and increase the resolution of heroin street purity and price. The Midwest currently has the highest concentration of purchase specimens with no known source based on forensic analyses.

New Data Systems and Analytical Methods to Address Gaps Should Be Developed and Implemented.

Implement National Recidivism Study (4.4.E.) The Bureau of Justice Statistics is currently completing analysis of data from its recently fielded national recidivism study. Data records for 70,000 prisoners are being compiled, with expected completion by the end of FY 2012. A final report is expected by spring of 2013.

Transition Drug Seizure Tracking to the National Seizure System (NSS) (7.2.B.) Electronic data from the Federal-wide Drug Seizure System (FDSS) and from other agency contributors has been obtained back to the year 2000, and is being de-duplicated and integrated into the NSS to provide accurate and comprehensive accounting of drug seizures. In addition, seizure records are being parsed and then aggregated to permit reporting of strategic seizure trends so that policymakers will be better informed on the latest trends and positioned to respond to vulnerabilities in illicit drug activities.

Enhance the Various Data that Inform Our Common Understanding of Global Illicit Drug Markets. (7.2.C.) Drug market data are improving in several areas. The Drug Enforcement Administration's Special Testing and Research Laboratory Carbon 14 analyses of cocaine samples, combined with the analysis of investigative and intelligence data, are improving understanding of the timing of the flow of cocaine to the United States. Increased sharing of data and methodology with the UN Office on Drugs and Crime (UNODC) is reducing the differences with the U.S. Government in estimates of illicit crop cultivation and potential production of illicit drugs. The Consolidated Counterdrug Database has been expanded to permit collection of data on the movement of Asian heroin and methamphetamine precursors, which will lay the groundwork for improved analysis of these trafficking patterns in coming years. Separately, in 2012, ONDCP will be updating estimates of the amount of drugs consumed in the United States. U.S. Government agencies will continue efforts to improve the CCDB by pursuing and implementing measures to increase efficiency and interagency participation. Similarly, they will continue to improve the Interagency Assessment of Cocaine Movement by refining its analytic methodologies.

In Coordination with Our International Partners, Improve Capacity for More Accurately, Rapidly, and Transparently Estimating the Cultivation and Yield of Marijuana, Opium, and Coca in the World. (7.2.D.) In November 2011, ONDCP coordinated a Federal Government effort with UNODC to reduce the major difference between the U.S. and UN cultivation estimates in Latin America, which derives from differing methodologies for accounting for aerial eradication. In a related effort, DEA conducted yield studies in Colombia and shared results with the Government of Colombia and UNODC. DEA began a year-long yield study in 2011 in Peru to update data that are 5 to 8 years old. The U.S. State Department participated in a coordination meeting in August 2011 led by UNODC and the Government of Afghanistan to discuss poppy cultivation and opium yields. The security situation in Afghanistan has made it difficult to develop accurate yield data; however, two U.S. expert agronomists were contracted by UNODC to provide recommendations to better estimate yield. Their report was submitted in October 2011 and UNODC is expected to apply the results in 2012.

Measures of Drug Use and Related Problems Must Be Useful at the State and Community Level

Support Innovative Criminal Justice Research Programs (4.1.C.) Probationers frequently violate their probation either through the use of drugs or by missing mandatory meetings. In 2004, Hawaii's Opportunity Probation with Enforcement (HOPE) program was launched to reduce probationer recidivism with swift, certain, and brief sanctions. In 2011, the National Institute of Justice funded a randomized controlled study to evaluate the HOPE program in selected communities. This study will determine whether the promising results obtained in Hawaii with HOPE can be replicated in other U.S. communities, thereby providing an effective alternative to incarceration.

Develop a Community Early Warning and Monitoring System that Tracks Substance Use and Problem Indicators at the Local Level (7.3.A.) SAMHSA has developed a plan to pilot test the program in a few selected communities to demonstrate the feasibility and utility of the concept. Meanwhile, SAMHSA continues to provide specialized reports from NSDUH on state and sub-state estimates, as well as special reports on selected metro areas and spotlights on emerging trends.

Conclusion

In addition to the information systems discussed previously, other data sources figure prominently in our efforts to reduce drug use and its consequences. For example, the National Vital Statistics System (NVSS) obtains data on all deaths occurring in the United States and is the source of data on deaths involving prescription drugs. NVSS data are based on death certificates filed in states and are obtained through a voluntary, cooperative relationship between the CDC National Center for Health Statistics (NCHS) and the states. NCHS has undertaken a number of preliminary efforts in recent years to promote state implementation of electronic registration systems, which are key to improving the timeliness, quality, and security of vital statistics data, including data on causes of death. To continue this effort and provide improved data related to deaths involving prescription drugs, the FY 2013 budget request includes essential funding to support efforts to begin to phase-in full implementation of electronic death records in as many states as possible.

The Administration will continue to support the maintenance and development of information systems critical to the formulation and assessment of drug control policies and programs. Only through the application of knowledge based upon sound scientific evidence obtained with such systems can effective programs and policies be designed, implemented, and assessed.

Policy Focus: Reducing Drugged Driving

Introduction

Thanks to increased public awareness and effective law enforcement, the United States has been able to successfully decrease the prevalence of drunk driving during the last several decades. However, drugged driving poses similar dangers on our Nation's roads. The Department of Transportation's most recent National Roadside Survey revealed that one in eight weekend night-time drivers tested positive for illegal drug use.[70] Fatality Analysis Reporting System (FARS) data shows that one in three deceased drivers with a known drug test tested positive for an illegal drug.[71]

In 2010 and 2011, President Obama declared the month of December *National Impaired Driving Prevention Month* and called on all Americans to commit to driving sober, drug free, and without distractions. The Administration's goal is to reduce the prevalence of drugged driving by 10 percent by 2015. To reach this mark, policy priorities must include preventive, environmental, and legal strategies.

Younger drivers appear to be especially affected by the dangers of drugged driving. Roughly 1 in 4 fatally injured drivers who tested positive for drugs were between the ages of 15 and 24, and half were younger than 35 years old.[72]

Marijuana is frequently involved in fatal traffic crashes and drugged driving in general. In 2009, marijuana accounted for 25 percent of all positive drug tests for fatally injured drivers and 43 percent among fatalities involving drivers 24 years of age and younger.[73] Moreover, approximately one in eight high school seniors responding to the 2011 Monitoring the Future Study (MTF) reported that in the 2 weeks prior to the survey interview they had driven after smoking marijuana.[74]

Accomplishments

Encourage States to Adopt *Per Se* Drug Impairment Laws (1.5.A.) The Administration encourages states to pursue enhanced legal responses, such as *per se* (or "zero tolerance") laws. Seventeen states already have *per se* statutes, and additional states should consider adopting these standards. These same standards have been applied to 12 million commercial drivers in the United States for the past two decades. The Administration has developed educational packets for states, providing them with information on the dangers of drugged driving and why *per se* laws are beneficial.

Collect Further Data on Drugged Driving (1.5.B.) NHTSA, with support from ONDCP, is currently planning the next iteration of the National Roadside Survey. Typically conducted every 10 years, NHTSA has accelerated the schedule so data will be available to assess the Nation's drugged driving goal in 2015. ONDCP and NHTSA are also currently supporting NIDA in driving simulator research to examine driving impairment as a result of marijuana and combined marijuana and alcohol use and correlate it with the results of oral fluid testing. NHTSA is conducting a study to estimate the risk of being involved in a crash after having consumed drugs, including both illegal drugs as well as prescription drugs. These research initiatives will enhance understanding of this emerging issue and guide policymakers moving forward.

Enhance Prevention of Drugged Driving by Educating Communities and Professionals (Action Item 1.5.C.) In October 2011, the Administration convened a drugged driving summit that brought together a wide coalition of stakeholders. The participants included prevention, youth-serving, and safety organizations; automobile and insurance industry representatives; and Federal agencies. During this summit, Mothers Against Drunk Driving (MADD) and the Administration announced an unprecedented partnership to raise public awareness regarding the consequences of drugged driving. MADD, which has successfully worked for decades to reduce drunk driving, has launched a national effort to provide support to the victims of poly-substance abuse (both alcohol and drugs) and drugged driving. Educating parents and youth about the dangers of drugged driving is an essential component to preventing drugged driving. It is vital that youth regularly hear about the consequences of drugged driving and that communities reinforce the message. To assist parents and communities, the Administration released a Drugged Driving Toolkit that provides tips for parents of teen drivers, sample community activities to raise public awareness, and resources to help teens reject negative influences. In the international arena, the United States increased public awareness of the threat of drugged driving through a resolution that was passed at the March 2011 meeting of the UN Commission on Narcotic Drugs and, as discussed previously, followed the resolution with a global research conference in Montreal in July 2011.

Provide Increased Training to Law Enforcement on Identifying Drugged Drivers (1.5.D.) Law enforcement plays a critical role in reducing drugged driving, and it is necessary to continue to provide training to officers to enable them to better identify and prosecute drugged driving. One such training program, Drug Evaluation and Classification (DEC), is funded by the Department of Transportation, National Highway Traffic Safety Administration (NHTSA), and managed and coordinated by the International Association of Chiefs of Police. A key part of DEC is the Drug Recognition Expert (DRE) program, which provides extensive training and certifies officers in detecting drugged driving. The number of states with certified DREs has continued to increase, and 49 of 50 States, plus the District of Columbia, currently have a certified DRE program. The Advanced Roadside Impaired Driving Enforcement program (ARIDE) is another training program that aids law enforcement in detecting drugged driving. ARIDE is a 16-hour training course for officers that have completed Standardized Field Sobriety Testing training, and it gives the officers additional skills to recognize signs and symptoms of drugs other than alcohol. The Administration currently is developing an online version of ARIDE to be complete in August 2012 that will make it more accessible to officers.

Develop Standard Screening Methodologies for Drug-Testing Labs To Use in Detecting the Presence of Drugs (1.5.E.) Improving standards and reliability for drug testing, including the development of a reliable and widely-available roadside test, is another important component to enforcing drugged driving laws. In 2011, the Administration committed to funding for the scientific determination for oral fluids testing as a complement to urine testing. HHS published a Federal Register notice requesting public comment on the scientific basis for oral fluid testing. HHS is moving forward to set standards for oral fluid testing that will be published in the future for public comment before they can be finalized in the Mandatory Guidelines for Drug Workplace Testing. These Guidelines will also be available for state and local jurisdictions to apply as appropriate for the prosecution of drugged driving violations, and to encourage the drug testing industry to develop accurate point-of-collection oral fluid testing devices.

Conclusion

Efforts at coordination and cooperation highlighted previously will be strengthened in 2012. The Administration will continue to reach out to tribal communities, prevention partners, health professionals, the business community, government agencies, and all levels of law enforcement to achieve the President's goal of reducing the prevalence of drugged driving by 10 percent by 2015.

Policy Focus: Preventing Prescription Drug Abuse

Introduction

While prescription drug abuse has been a major public health concern for several years, the public health and public safety consequences of prescription drug abuse continue to mount. National data show that in 2009 the 39,147 drug-induced deaths exceeded deaths from motor vehicle crashes (36,216).[75] In 2008, the latest year for which national data are available, there were 20,044 unintentional prescription drug overdose deaths.[76] The problem of prescription drug abuse is particularly acute in the southern United States and the Appalachian region.[77] Prescription drugs caused an average of seven deaths per day in Florida in 2010, according to the Florida Medical Examiners Commission Drug Report.[78]

The cost in human lives lost to prescription drug abuse is tragic and cannot be overstated for the families and friends that have experienced the loss of a loved one. Yet there is also a cost to society at large. A recent study estimated that the health care, workforce, and criminal justice costs of prescription drug abuse amounted to $55.7 billion in 2007, the last year for which data are available.[79] Financial consequences are just part of the damage caused by prescription drug abuse. Substance use disorders, whether caused by an addiction to painkillers or other illegal drugs, can tear families apart and damage lives.

One of the most disturbing trends to emerge is the number of young people initiating their drug use with prescription medications containing controlled substances. The ready availability of prescription drugs and lack of understanding about the risks of prescription drug abuse have contributed to continued high rates of youth use. While marijuana remains the most common illegal drug of first use by individuals aged 12 or older, in 2010, one in four people using drugs for the first time began by using a prescription drug non-medically.[80] The vast majority of individuals reporting that they have intentionally misused prescription drugs (71 percent) state that they obtained the drug from a friend or a relative.[81]

Faced with the seriousness of the prescription drug abuse problem, the Administration issued its *Prescription Drug Abuse Prevention Plan* in April 2011. This chapter provides an overview of the Plan, as well as an update on accomplishments to date.

Accomplishments

The Administration's approach to reducing prescription drug abuse contains four main elements: educating prescribers, parents, and patients; increasing the number of prescription drug monitoring programs and improving their effectiveness; encouraging and providing for the proper disposal of prescription drugs; and increasing enforcement against illicit pill mills, prescribing that is not in keeping with standard medical practices, and doctor shopping.

Education: The Administration's plan for reducing prescription drug abuse calls for all prescribers to be trained in proper opioid prescribing practices. It also calls for an effort to educate parents and patients on the importance of securing medications and using medications only as directed. Many prescribers do not receive substance use disorder education when they are in professional schools. This is illustrated by the fact that a 2000 survey found that 56 percent of physician residency programs required training in substance use disorders and the median number of curricular hours ranges from 3 to 12 hours.[82] Three states—Iowa, Massachusetts and Utah—saw the need for advanced training in prescribing opioids and passed legislation requiring prescriber education. In these states, an individual prescriber must take a course to obtain or renew their license. In the course, the prescriber is trained regarding the appropriate prescribing of pain medications and counseling patients on proper storage and the addictive potential of the medications.

Naloxone, an overdose-reversing medication, provides an additional area of public education that may help reduce overdose deaths caused by the non-medical use of prescription drugs. ONDCP, CDC, and SAMHSA are working with first responders to identify and address any gaps in training, access, and use of naloxone by first responders. In 2012, ONDCP will participate in a public workshop conducted by the Food and Drug Administration at which the medical and social issues related to naloxone use by non-medical personnel will be discussed. In addition, guidance will be provided to researchers, community groups, and the pharmaceutical industry on potential routes for marketing approval for novel naloxone formulations.

Educate Physicians about Opiate Painkiller Prescribing (2.2.A.) In 2011, SAMHSA conducted online training on prescription drug abuse for physicians and provided technical assistance on the topic. More than 2,600 of the approximately 3,200 physicians participating in the online courses received continuing medical education credits. Additionally, SAMHSA conducted in-person training for physicians in 19 states with high rates of prescription drug abuse.

Monitoring: Prescription drug monitoring programs (PDMPs) are now authorized in 48 states and only two states (Missouri and New Hampshire) and the District of Columbia lack legislation authorizing a PDMP. States such as Maryland, Georgia, and Arkansas recently passed legislation to establish PDMPs. In addition, states are beginning to share data across state lines. Ohio and Kentucky successfully shared data in a test pilot and many other states are expected to increase their data sharing capabilities over the next several months. PDMPs now play a crucial role in reducing prescription drug abuse, and the Administration is committed to ensuring that they continue to operate, are enhanced, and are adequately funded. The FY 2012 Department of Justice budget included $7 million to fund PDMPs. Recently, legislative language was included in the FY 2012 appropriations bill that allows the Department of Veterans Affairs (VA) to share data with state PDMPs. This issue was identified in the Administration's *Prescription Drug Abuse Prevention Plan*, and removing this prohibition will allow for an important patient safety tool to be made available to veterans. The Department of Veterans Affairs is developing regulations to implement VA participation in state PDMPs. ONDCP, along with the Department of Health and Human Services and other partners, is also looking to connect health information technology with PDMPs, an effort that will jumpstart efforts to make PDMP data more accessible to prescribers.

Disposal: As stated previously, 71 percent of individuals that reported that they had misused prescription drugs obtained the drugs from a friend or relative.[84] This demonstrates the importance of getting these unneeded or expired prescription drugs out of the home and properly disposed where they cannot harm people or the environment.

The Secure and Responsible Drug Disposal Act of 2010 allowed for DEA to implement regulations on the disposal of controlled substances by ultimate users, long term care facilities, and other authorized persons. Until the regulations are promulgated, DEA will arrange for communities to get rid of unneeded or expired prescription drugs through National Prescription Drug Take Back Days. These Take Back Days have been one of the most successful aspects of the *Prescription Drug Abuse Prevention Plan*. As of December 2011, three Take Back Days have resulted in the collection and destruction of more than 498 tons of medications through this initiative. The success of this initiative could not have been accomplished without the combined efforts of more than 3,900 Federal, state, local, and tribal law enforcement agencies that sponsored more than 5,000 collection sites.

Enforcement: The fourth pillar of the Administration's plan to reduce prescription drug abuse is law enforcement. Not only have law enforcement professionals been trained on putting together effective diversion cases, but several multi-agency operations have been carried out to shut down pill mills and arrest prescribers engaged in illegal activity.

Florida has long been the epicenter of rogue pharmacies and illicit pain clinics. In February 2011, the DEA, working with state and local counterparts, took action in Operation Pill Nation I to crack down on pill mill operations in southern Florida. Indictments have been brought against doctors and others involved in these illegal operations that fed the addiction of individuals in Florida, as well as in the Appalachian region and other areas of the eastern seaboard. In October 2011, DEA's Operation Pill Nation II resulted in 22 arrests in Orlando and Tampa, Florida as part of the continuing effort to reduce the number of rogue pharmacies and illicit pain clinics in the State. DEA targeted rogue pharmacies and illicit pain clinics in South Florida through the use of twelve Tactical Diversion Squads during Operation Pill Nation, leading to the closure of forty "pain clinics" and the seizure of more than $18.9 million in cash and assets. DEA is expanding the number of Tactical Diversion Squads across the United States. Investigations conducted by DEA Tactical Diversion Squads and HIDTA Task Force groups will help reduce the number of illicit pain clinics as well as other criminal schemes designed to divert controlled substance pharmaceuticals for non-medical use.

HIDTA is also addressing prescription drug diversion on the Federal, state, and local levels. Many HIDTA-designated counties are in areas hard hit by prescription drug abuse. Adams and Scioto Counties in Ohio, two areas that have been particularly affected by the prescription drug abuse epidemic, were recently added to the Ohio HIDTA. This designation will help law enforcement officials in these two counties bring additional resources to bear on the prescription drug abuse problem. In addition, the HIDTA-funded National Methamphetamine and Pharmaceutical Initiative trains law enforcement professionals in effective investigation and enforcement techniques for pharmaceutical drug cases.

Conclusion

The Administration has established a bold five-year goal–a 15 percent reduction in non-medical use of prescription-type psychotherapeutic drugs in the past year among people 12 years of age and older. Accomplishing this goal will take the cooperation of Federal agencies, state and local government, parents, prescribers, and patients.

Conclusion

The progress depicted in the preceding pages demonstrates the Administration's ongoing commitment to the goals, principles, and actions articulated in the President's first *National Drug Control Strategy*. Further progress in implementing the *Strategy* will require a comprehensive effort that includes Federal, state, local, tribal, and territorial government agencies, international institutions and partner nations, nongovernmental organizations, academia, private industry, and American citizens from all walks of life.

In particular, a continuing partnership with Congress will be essential to sustain our progress, make necessary adjustments and enhancements, and respond quickly to changing trends and emerging threats. This relationship has already produced important results. With the enactment and retroactive application of the Fair Sentencing Act, the disparity in sentencing between offenses for crack cocaine and powder cocaine has been drastically reduced, ensuring more fair and effective application of the law. The passage of the Second Chance Act has underscored the importance of substance abuse treatment, employment, mentoring, and other services that improve the transition of individuals from the criminal justice system to a new life in the community. The Secure and Responsible Drug Disposal Act of 2010 will allow the DEA to make it easier for Americans to dispose of unused controlled substances and thereby prevent prescription drug abuse. The Synthetic Drug Control Act of 2011, passed by the House of Representatives in December 2011, will help to protect young people from the emergence of synthetic drugs of abuse such as so-called 'bath salts' and 'legal' marijuana products like K2 and Spice. Continuing support in Congress for the Merida Initiative and related international programs has proven vital in assisting our partners in the Western Hemisphere to combat transnational organized crime and reduce drug production and trafficking. And the FY 2012 Appropriations bill included language that will now allow information sharing between the Veterans Administration and state PDMPs, while also providing important funding support to many of the key priorities in the President's National Drug Control Budget. The Department of Veterans Affairs is developing regulations to implement VA participation in state PDMPs.

Moving forward, we will work throughout 2012 to implement the full range of actions in the *National Drug Control Strategy*, with special emphasis on a number of priority areas. We will work to maintain our prevention and treatment efforts, ensuring continued dissemination of effective prevention messages and further integrating drug treatment services into the public health system. We will focus on supporting recovery by increasing public awareness, developing the necessary support systems, and working to eliminate legal and regulatory barriers. We will move forward with implementing the *Prescription Drug Abuse Prevention Plan* and continue to pursue legislative, law enforcement, and research initiatives aimed at reducing drugged driving.

The Administration will continue to promote criminal justice reform and innovative public safety interventions that ensure fairness, save tax dollars, treat addiction, and reduce criminal recidivism. Our international efforts will focus on the Western Hemisphere, maintaining our support for Mexico, Colombia, and our other partners in the Andes, Central America, and the Caribbean. Legalization of drugs will not be considered in this approach. Making drugs more available and more accessible will not reduce drug use and its adverse consequences for public health and safety. We will continue to educate young people and all Americans about the science on the harmful health effects of marijuana use.

Illicit drug use represents a significant threat to our Nation's health, safety, and economic competitiveness. Sustained investment in effective programs along the entire spectrum of prevention, early intervention, treatment, recovery, criminal justice, domestic law enforcement, and international cooperation will remain essential if we seek to reduce the enormous costs that illegal drug use imposes on American society. In 2012, the Administration looks forward to a continued partnership with Congress and the American people in addressing a problem that affects nearly every aspect of our national life.

List of Acronyms

ARIDE	Advanced Roadside Impaired Driving Enforcement
ATI	Above the Influence
BCSC	Bulk Cash Smuggling Center
BJA	Bureau of Justice Assistance
CADCA	Community Anti-Drug Coalitions of America
CBSI	Caribbean Basin Security Initiative
CCDB	Consolidated Counterdrug Data Base
CDC	Centers for Disease Control and Prevention
CND	Commission on Narcotic Drugs
CNWG	Counternarcotics Working Group
CPOT	Consolidated Priority Operational Target
CSAT	Center for Substance Abuse Treatment
DASIS	Drug and Alcohol Services Information System
DAWN	Drug Abuse Warning Network
DEA	Drug Enforcement Administration
DEC	Drug Evaluation and Classification
DFC	Drug Free Communities
DMI	Drug Market Intervention
DoD	U.S. Department of Defense
DRE	Drug Recognition Expert
EPIC	El Paso Intelligence Center
FARS	Fatality Analysis Reporting System
FBI	Federal Bureau of Investigation
FDSS	Federal-wide Drug Seizure System
HIDTA	High Intensity Drug Trafficking Area
HIV	Human Immunodeficiency Virus
HOPE	Hawaii's Opportunity Probation with Enforcement or Honest Opportunity Probation with Enforcement

HRSA	Health Resources and Services Administration
HSI	Homeland Security Investigations
HUD	U.S. Department of Housing and Urban Development
IACM	Interagency Assessment of Cocaine Movement
ICE	U.S. Immigration and Customs Enforcement
INCSR	International Narcotics Control Strategy Report
I-SATS	Inventory of Substance Abuse Treatment Services
JIATF	Joint Interagency Task Force
MADD	Mothers Against Drunk Driving
NDIC	National Drug Intelligence Center
NHTSA	National Highway Traffic Safety Administration
NIDA	National Institute on Drug Abuse
NSDUH	National Survey on Drug Use and Health
NSS	National Seizure System
OAS/CICAD	Organization of American States/Inter-American Drug Abuse Control Commission
OCDETF	Organized Crime Drug Enforcement Task Force
ODNI	Office of the Director of National Intelligence
OJJDP	Office of Juvenile Justice and Delinquency Prevention
ONDCP	Office of National Drug Control Policy
PACT	Police and Communities Together
PDMP	Prescription Drug Monitoring Program
PHA	Public Housing Authority
PRO-ACT	Pennsylvania Recovery Organization - Achieving Community Together
RCSP	Recovery Community Services Program
ROSC	Recovery Oriented Systems of Care
SAMHSA	Substance Abuse and Mental Health Services Administration
SAPTBG	Substance Abuse Prevention and Treatment Block Grant
SBIRT	Screening, Brief Intervention, and Referral to Treatment
TCE	Targeted Capacity Expansion
TEDS	Treatment Episode Data Set

UN	United Nations
UNODC	United Nations Office on Drugs and Crime
USAID	United States Agency for International Development
VA	U.S. Department of Veterans Affairs
VTC	Veterans Treatment Court
WASBIRT	Washington State Screening, Brief Intervention, and Referral to Treatment

References

1. Johnston, L. D., O'Malley, P. M., Bachman, J. G., & Schulenberg, J. E. (2011). "Marijuana use continues to rise among U.S. teens, while alcohol use hits historic lows." University of Michigan News Service: Ann Arbor, MI. Retrieved from http://www.monitoringthefuture.org

2. Johnston, L. D., O'Malley, P. M., Bachman, J. G., & Schulenberg, J. E. (2011). "Marijuana use continues to rise among U.S. teens, while alcohol use hits historic lows." University of Michigan News Service: Ann Arbor, MI. Retrieved from http://www.monitoringthefuture.org

3. American Association of Poison Control Centers. (2012). Synthetic marijuana data, updated January 5, 2012. Retrieved from http://www.aapcc.org/dnn/Portals/0/Synthetic%20Marijuana%20Data%20for%20Website%20 1 5.2012.pdf

4. Centers for Disease Control and Prevention. (2010). 2009 Youth risk behavior survey fact sheet on alcohol and other drug use and academic achievement. Atlanta, GA. Retrieved from http://www.cdc.gov/HealthyYouth/health_ and_academics/#1

5. Bray, R., Marsden, M.E., Herbold, J., Peterson, M. (1992). Progress toward eliminating drug and alcohol abuse among U.S. military personnel. *Armed Forces and Society, 18(4)*, 476-496.

6. Office of National Drug Control Policy. (2011). Arrestee drug abuse monitoring program: 2010 annual report. Washington, DC. Retrieved from http://www.whitehouse.gov/sites/default/files/ondcp/policy-and-research/adam2010. pdf

7. National Center for Statistics and Analysis. (2010). Traffic safety facts: Drug involvement of fatally injured drivers. (DOT HS 811 415). Washington, DC: National Highway Traffic Safety Administration. Retrieved from http://www-nrd.nhtsa.dot.gov/Pubs/811415.pdf

8. National Drug Intelligence Center. (2011). The economic impact of illicit drug use on American society. Washington, D.C.: United States Department of Justice. Retrieved from http://www.justice.gov/ndic/ pubs44/44731/44731p.pdf

9. Miller, T., & Hendrie, D. (2009). Substance abuse prevention dollars and cents: a cost-benefit analysis. DHHS Pub. No. (SMA) 07-4298. Rockville, MD: Center for Substance Abuse Prevention, Substance Abuse and Mental Health Services Administration.

10. Johnston, L. D., O'Malley, P. M., Bachman, J. G., & Schulenberg, J. E. (2011). "Marijuana use continues to rise among U.S. teens, while alcohol use hits historic lows." University of Michigan News Service: Ann Arbor, MI. Retrieved from http://www.monitoringthefuture.org

11. Johnston, L. D., O'Malley, P. M., Bachman, J. G., & Schulenberg, J. E. (2011). "Marijuana use continues to rise among U.S. teens, while alcohol use hits historic lows." University of Michigan News Service: Ann Arbor, MI. Retrieved from http://www.monitoringthefuture.org

12. Johnston, L. D., O'Malley, P. M., Bachman, J. G., & Schulenberg, J. E. (2011). "Marijuana use continues to rise among U.S. teens, while alcohol use hits historic lows." University of Michigan News Service: Ann Arbor, MI. Retrieved from http://www.monitoringthefuture.org

13. Johnston, L. D., O'Malley, P. M., Bachman, J. G., & Schulenberg, J. E. (2011). Monitoring the future national results on adolescent drug use: Overview of key findings, 2010. Ann Arbor, MI: Institute for Social Research, The University of Michigan. Retrieved from: http://monitoringthefuture.org/pubs/monographs/mtf-overview2010.pdf

14. Substance Abuse and Mental Health Services Administration. (2011). Results from the 2010 national survey on drug use and health: National findings. Office of Applied Studies, NSDUH Series H-41, HHS Publication No. (SMA) 11-4658. Rockville, MD. Retrieved from http://oas.samhsa.gov/NSDUH/2k10NSDUH/2k10Results.htm

15. Spoth, R., Redmond, C., Clair, S., Shin, C., Greenberg, M., & Feinberg, M. (2011). Preventing substance misuse through community–university partnerships: Randomized controlled trial outcomes 4½ years past baseline. *American Journal of Preventive Medicine, 40(4)*, 440-447.

16. Hawkins, J., Oesterle, S., Brown, E., Arthur, M., Abbott, R., Fagan, A., & Catalano, R. (2009). Results of a type 2 translational research trial to prevent adolescent drug use and delinquency: A test of communities that care. *Arch Pediatr Adolesc Med, 163(9)*, 789-798.

17.   Substance Abuse and Mental Health Services Administration. Fiscal year 2011 justification of estimates for appropriations committees: online performance appendix. Retrieved from http://www.samhsa.gov/Budget/FY2011/SAMHSA_FY11CJ.pdf

18.   Safe Schools/Healthy Students Program. Government Performance and Results Act Data.

19.   Substance Abuse and Mental Health Services Administration. (2008). Drug-free workplace: A kit. Retrieved from http://www.workplace.samhsa.gov/wpworkit/index.html

20.   ICF International. (2011). Drug-free communities support program national evaluation: 2010 status report. Report prepared for the Office of National Drug Control Policy. Fairfax, VA. Retrieved from http://www.whitehouse.gov/sites/default/files/ondcp/grants-content/dfc_2010_status_report_final.pdf

21.   The White House. (2011). Strengthening our military families: Meeting America's commitment. Retrieved from http://www.defense.gov/home/features/2011/0111_initiative/Strengthening_our_Military_January_2011.pdf

22.   National Center for Veterans Analysis and Statistics (NCVAS). (2011). Veteran population. U.S. Department of Veterans Affairs. Retrieved from http://www.va.gov/vetdata/Veteran_Population.asp

23.   Eggleston, A. M., Straits-Troster, K., & Kudler, H. (2009). Substance use treatment needs among recent veterans. *North Carolina Medical Journal, 70*, 48-54.

24.   Slater, M. D., Kelly, K. J., Stanley, L. R., Lawrence, F. R., & Comello, M. L. G. (2011). Assessing media campaigns linking marijuana non-use with autonomy and aspirations: 'Be under your own influence' and ONDCP's 'above the influence'. *Prevention Science, 12(1),* 12-22.

25.   Carpenter, C. S., & Pechmann, C. (2011). Exposure to the above the influence antidrug advertisements and adolescent marijuana use in the United States, 2006-2008. *American Journal of Public Health, 101,* 948-954.

26.   Scheier, L. M., Grenard, J. L., & Holtz, K. D. (2011). An empirical assessment of the above the influence advertising campaign. *J. Drug Education, 41(4),* 431-461.

27.   Bernstein, J., Bernstein, E., Tassiopoulos, K., Heeren, T., Levenson, S., & Hingson, R. (2005). Brief motivational intervention at a clinic visit reduces cocaine and heroin use. *Drug and Alcohol Dependence, 77,* 49-59.

28.   Estee, S., He, L., Mancuso, D., & Felver, B. (2006). Medicaid cost outcomes. Department of Social and Health Services, Research and Data Analysis Division: Olympia, Washington.

29.   Estee, S., Wickizer, T., He, L., Shah, M. F., & Mancuso, D. (2010). Evaluation of the Washington State screening, brief intervention, and referral to treatment project: cost outcomes for Medicaid patients screened in hospital emergency departments. *Medical Care, 48(1),* 18-24.

30.   Ondersma, S. J., Svikis, D. S., & Schuster, C. R. (2007). Computer-based brief intervention: A randomized trial with postpartum women. *American Journal of Preventive Medicine, 32(3),* 231-8.

31.   Substance Abuse and Mental Health Services Administration. FY 2011 SAMHSA Grant Awards: CSAT / TI-11-005: Cooperative agreements for screening, brief intervention and referral to treatment (Short Title: SBIRT). Retrieved from http://www.samhsa.gov/grants/2011/awards/ti_11_005.aspx

32.   Wagner, C. L., Katikaneni, L. D., Cox, T. H., & Ryan, R. M. (1998). The impact of prenatal drug exposure on the neonate. *Obstet Gynecol Clin North Am, 25,* 169–94.

33.   National Center on Substance Abuse and Child Welfare. Substance exposed infants. Retrieved from http://www.ncsacw.samhsa.gov/resources/substance-exposed-infants.aspx

34.   American College of Obstetricians and Gynecologists. (2008). At-risk drinking and illicit drug use: Ethical issues in obstetric and gynecologic practice. ACOG Committee Opinion No.422. *Obstet Gynecol, 112,* 1449–60.

35.   American College of Obstetricians and Gynecologists. (2011). At-risk drinking and alcohol dependence: obstetric and gynecologic implications. Committee Opinion No. 496. *Obstet Gynecol, 118,* 383–8.

36.   Young, N. K., Gardner, S., Otero, C., Dennis, K., Chang, R., Earle, K., & Amatetti, S. (2009). Substance-exposed infants: State responses to the problem. HHS Pub. No. (SMA) 09-4369. Rockville, MD: Substance Abuse and Mental Health Services Administration.

37.   Ettner, S. L., Huang, D., Evans, E., Ash, D. R., Hardy, M., Jourabchi, M., & Hser, Y. I. (2006). Benefit-cost in the California treatment outcome project: Does substance abuse treatment 'pay or itself'? *Health Services Research, 41(1),* 192-213.

38.   Wickizer, T. M., Krupski, A., Stark, M. D., Mancuso, D., & Campbell, K. (2006). The effect of substance abuse treatment on medicaid expenditures among general assistance welfare clients in Washington State. *The Milbank Quarterly, 84(3),* 555-576.

39. Estee, S., & Nordlund, D. J. (2003). Washington State supplemental security income (SSI) cost-offset pilot project: 2002 progress report. Washington State Department of Social and Health Services.

40. Substance Abuse and Mental Health Services Administration. (2011). Results from the 2010 national survey on drug use and health: National findings. Office of Applied Studies, NSDUH Series H-41, HHS Publication No. (SMA) 11-4658. Rockville, MD. Retrieved from http://oas.samhsa.gov/NSDUH/2k10NSDUH/2k10Results.htm

41. U.S. Department of Health and Human Services. (2011). Determination that a demonstration needle exchange program would be effective in reducing drug abuse and the risk of acquired immune deficiency syndrome infection among intravenous drug users. Retrieved from http://www.federalregister.gov/articles/2011/02/23/2011-3990/determination-that-a-demonstration-needle-exchange-program-would-be-effective-in-reducing-drug-abuse.

42. Bureau of Justice Statistics. (2011). Key facts at a glance: Correctional populations. U.S. Department of Justice. Retrieved from http://bjs.ojp.usdoj.gov/content/glance/tables/corr2tab.cfm

43. National Association of State Budget Officers. (1989). Fiscal year 1988 state expenditure report. 71. Retrieved from www.nasbo.org/Publications/StateExpenditureReport/StateExpenditureReportArchives/tabid/107/Default.aspx

44. National Association of State Budget Officers. (2011). Fiscal year 2010 state expenditure report. 52. Retrieved from www.nasbo.org/Publications/StateExpenditureReport/tabid/79/Default.aspx

45. Bureau of Justice Statistics. (2011). Correctional populations in the United States, 2010. U S. Department of Justice. Retrieved from http://bjs.ojp.usdoj.gov/content/pub/pdf/cpus10.pdf

46. Bureau of Justice Statistics. (2007). Drug use and dependence, state and federal prisoners, 2004. U.S. Department of Justice. Retrieved from http://bjs.ojp.usdoj.gov/content/pub/pdf/dudsfp04.pdf

47. Bureau of Justice Statistics. (2007). Drug use and dependence, state and Federal prisoners, 2004. U.S. Department of Justice. Retrieved from http://bjs.ojp.usdoj.gov/content/pub/pdf/dudsfp04.pdf

48. Bureau of Justice Statistics. (2011). Prisoners in 2010. U S. Department of Justice. Retrieved from http://bjs.ojp.usdoj.gov/content/pub/pdf/p10.pdf

49. Beck, A. J. (2006). The importance of successful reentry to jail population growth. [PowerPoint slides]. Retrieved from http://urban.org/projects/reentry-roundtable/upload/beck.PPT

50. Langan, P. A., & Levin, D. J. (2002). Recidivism of prisoners released in 1994. NCJ 1934427. Washington, DC: U.S. Department of Justice, Bureau of Justice Statistics. Retrieved from http://bjs.ojp.usdoj.gov/content/pub/pdf/rpr94.pdf

51. ONDCP calculation based on data from: Guerino, P., Harrison, P. M., & Sabol, W. J. (2011). Prisoners in 2010. Washington, DC: U.S. Department of Justice, Bureau of Justice Statistics. Retrieved from http://bjs.ojp.usdoj.gov/content/pub/pdf/p10.pdf

52. The following sites received training: Flint, Michigan; Guntersville, Alabama; Jacksonville, Florida; Lake County (Gary), Indiana; Montgomery County (Damascus), Maryland; New Orleans, Louisiana; and Roanoke, Virginia.

53. National Association of Drug Court Professionals. (2010). Veterans treatment courts. Retrieved from http://www.nadcp.org/sites/default/files/nadcp/VTC%20Brief.pdf

54. National Association of Drug Court Professionals. (2010). Veterans treatment courts. Retrieved from http://www.nadcp.org/sites/default/files/nadcp/VTC%20Brief.pdf

55. Federal Interagency Reentry Council. (2011). Reentry mythbuster: On veterans benefits. National Reentry Resource Center. Retrieved from http://www.nationalreentryresourcecenter.org/documents/0000/1084/Reentry_Council_Mythbuster_VA.pdf

56. Rossman, S. B., Roman, J., Zweig, J. M., Rempel, M., & Lindquist, C. (2011). The multi-site adult drug court evaluation: Executive summary. Urban Institute. Retrieved from https://www.ncjrs.gov/pdffiles1/nij/grants/237108.pdf

57. U.S. Department of Justice National Drug Intelligence Center. (2011). National drug threat assessment 2011. Retrieved from http://www.justice.gov/ndic/pubs44/44849/44849p.pdf

58. Johnston, L. D., O'Malley, P. M., Bachman, J. G., & Schulenberg, J. E. (2011). "Marijuana use continues to rise among U.S. teens, while alcohol use hits historic lows." University of Michigan News Service: Ann Arbor, MI. Retrieved from http://www.monitoringthefuture.org

59. National Association for Model State Drug Laws. (2011). Cathinones—state legislative update (current as of December 2011). Retrieved from http://namsdl.org/documents/billstatusreportcathinones12.19.2011.pdf

60. National Association for Model State Drug Laws. (2011). Synthetic cannabinoids—state legislative update (current as of December 2011). Retrieved from http://namsdl.org/documents/BillStatusReportSyntheticCannabinoids12.19.2011.pdf

61. The annual potential production estimates for each country cultivating significant amounts of illicit coca and poppy are presented in annual briefings by the U.S. Government intelligence community. These unpublished presentations provide the figures used to calculate the potential production numbers for each growing area. Those data include net cultivation, leaf production, and the crop yield and processing efficiencies.

62. U.S. Department of State. (2012). International narcotics control strategy report. Washington, DC. Retrieved from http://www.state.gov/j/inl/rls/nrcrpt/2012/vol1/184098.htm#Colombia

63. For more information on cocaine production and movement, see Office of National Drug Control Policy. (2012). Cocaine smuggling in 2010. Washington, DC. Retrieved from http://www.whitehouse.gov/ondcp/transit-zone-operations/cocainesmuggling2010

64. Substance Abuse and Mental Health Services Administration. (2011). Results from the 2010 national survey on drug use and health: National findings. (Office of Applied Studies, NSDUH Series H-41, HHS Publication No. (SMA) 11-4658. Rockville, MD. Retrieved from http://oas.samhsa.gov/NSDUH/2k10NSDUH/2k10Results.htm

65. Office of National Drug Control Policy. (2011). Arrestee drug abuse monitoring program: 2010 annual report. Executive Office of the President: Washington, DC. Available at http://www.whitehouse.gov/sites/default/files/ondcp/policy-and-research/adam2010.pdf

66. Quest Diagnostics Incorporated. (2011). Quest diagnostics drug testing index™. Madison, NJ. Retrieved from http://www.questdiagnostics.com/employersolutions/dti/2011_09/dti.pdf

67. Special Inspector General for Afghanistan Reconstruction. (2012). Quarterly report to the Congress. Retrieved from http://www.sigar.mil/pdf/quarterlyreports/Jan2012/Lores%20PDF/2012JanBook.pdf

68. U.S. Department of State. (2011). International narcotics control strategy report. Washington, DC. Retrieved from http://www.state.gov/g/inl/rls/nrcrpt/2011/vol1/156362.htm#peru

69. U.S. Government estimates (last updated August 2011).

70. Lacey, J. H., Kelly-Baker, T., Furr-Holden, D., Voas, R. B., Romano, E., Ramirez, A., Brainard, C. M., Torres, P., & Berning, A. (2009). 2007 national roadside survey of alcohol and drug use by drivers: Drug results (DOT HS 811 249). Washington, DC: National Highway Traffic Safety Administration.

71. National Highway Traffic Safety Administration. (2010). Traffic safety facts: Drug involvement of fatally injured drivers (DOT HS 811 415). Washington, D.C.: National Center for Statistics and Analysis.

72. Office of National Drug Control Policy. (2011). Drug testing and drug-involved driving of fatally injured drivers in the United States: 2005-2009. Washington, D.C.: Executive Office of the President.

73. Office of National Drug Control Policy. (2011). Drug testing and drug-involved driving of fatally injured drivers in the United States: 2005-2009. Washington, D.C.: Executive Office of the President.

74. Unpublished data from the 2011 Monitoring the Future Study.

75. National Center for Health Statistics. (2012). National vital statistics reports: Deaths: Final Data for 2009. NVSR Volume 60, No. 3. Washington, D.C.: Centers for Disease Control and Prevention.

76. Centers for Disease Control and Prevention. (2011) MMWR weekly, vital signs: Overdoses of prescription opioid pain relievers—United States, 1999-2008. Retrieved from http://www.cdc.gov/mmwr/preview/mmwrhtml/mm6043a4.htm

77. Centers for Disease Control and Prevention. (November 2011). Vital signs. Retrieved from http://www.cdc.gov/vitalsigns/PainkillerOverdoses/#StateInfo

78. Florida Department of Law Enforcement. (2011). Drugs identified in deceased persons by Florida medical examiners, 2010 report.

79. Birnbaum H. G., White, A. G., Schiller, M., Waldman, T., Cleveland, J. M., & Roland, C. L. (2011). Societal costs of prescription opioid abuse, dependence, and misuse in the United States. Pain Medicine, 12, 657-667.

80. Substance Abuse and Mental Health Services Administration. (2011). Results from the 2010 national survey on drug use and health: National findings. Office of Applied Studies, NSDUH Series H-41, HHS Publication No. (SMA) 11-4658. Rockville, MD. Retrieved from http://oas.samhsa.gov/NSDUH/2k10NSDUH/2k10Results.htm

81. Substance Abuse and Mental Health Services Administration. (2011). Results from the 2010 national survey on drug use and health: National findings. Office of Applied Studies, NSDUH Series H-41, HHS Publication No. (SMA) 11-4658. Rockville, MD. Retrieved from http://oas.samhsa.gov/NSDUH/2k10NSDUH/2k10Results.htm

82. Isaacson, J. H., Fleming, M., Kraus, M., Kahn, R., & Mundt, M. (2000). A national survey of training in substance use disorders in residency programs. J Stud Alcohol. 61(6), 912-915.

83. Kim, D., Irwin, K. S., & Khoshnood, K. (2009). Expanded access to naloxone: Options for critical response to the epidemic of opioid overdose mortality. American Journal of Public Health, 99(3), 402-407.

84. Substance Abuse and Mental Health Services Administration. (2011). Results from the 2010 national survey on drug use and health: National findings. Office of Applied Studies, NSDUH Series H-41, HHS Publication No. (SMA) 11-4658. Rockville, MD. Retrieved from http://oas.samhsa.gov/NSDUH/2k10NSDUH/2k10Results.htm